# BEYOND PLAGUE URBANISM

# Beyond Plague Urbanism

ANDY MERRIFIELD

MONTHLY REVIEW PRESS

*New York*

Library of Congress Cataloging-in-Publication Data
available from the publisher.

ISBN: 978-168590-013-7 cloth

Typeset in Bulmer MT

Monthly Review Press | New York
www.monthlyreview.org

5 4 3 2 1

"Toto, I have a feeling we're not in Kansas any more...."

—DOROTHY, ARRIVING IN OZ, EPIGRAPH TO
THOMAS PYNCHON'S "INTO THE ZONE," *GRAVITY'S RAINBOW*

## 1

IT HADN'T RAINED FOR WEEKS, but rainbows beamed in the sunshine. Rainbows painted by kids, taped to windows, facing outward to the world, for passers-by to see. "*After the storm comes a . . .*," said one caption, above an especially vivid rainbow. Now, much as I love rainbows, smiled each time I saw one, in lockdown Britain, none allayed my unease. Daily the body count topped a thousand. Venturing outdoors became evermore nerve-wracking. To avoid people, I crossed the street, veered off the sidewalk, pitted myself against oncoming traffic. Blind corners menaced. Someone creeping up on me, getting too close, terrified. Supermarket runs brought on the jitters. Soon all outside contact tormented, unleashed an agoraphobic paranoia. I knew I wasn't alone feeling this. My left eyelid started to twitch. I began sleeping badly. When I did drop off, wild, surreal dreams plagued my slumber.

I'm not sure when it dawned, when I chose to confront the tug I felt each day, that warping of time and space. I'm not sure when I decided to defy gravity. Defying gravity meant journeying over the rainbow—*Gravity's Rainbow*, Thomas Pynchon's novelistic masterpiece from 1973. His rainbow had been there all along, on my bookshelf for more than thirty years, lying unread. I'd heard plenty these days about virtual reading groups tackling *Moby-Dick*, discussing Ahab's monomania alongside the president's. But Melville's Great White isn't a patch on Pynchon's V2. G.R.

For here was a book, and a man, for our times, a maestro. He'd made self-isolation a life-form, paranoia a permanent mode of being, quarantining himself for a half-century or more, avoiding everybody in his splendid velvet underground. I remember the old days when I lived in my broom closet of an apartment on Manhattan's Upper West Side, wandering out without fearing crowds, happily strolling down Broadway to Zabar's. Back then I thought I'd even discovered where the great recluse hung out, on West 81st Street, twelve blocks down from me. Although it's only now, years later, amid a pandemic, reflecting upon writing a book about this pandemic, about what it means for our cities, that I seem ready to deal with Pynchon's rainbow, to enter his Zone and really *get it*, to finally feel its curve, unmistakably.

They say you can't hear the killing, that it's a silent death. If you hear the explosion, you're still alive—this time. But what about the next time, the next one to drop? Early in *Gravity's Rainbow*, the mad neurologist Doctor Spectro explains, "Imagine a missile one hears approaching only *after* it explodes. The blast of the rocket, falling faster than sound—then growing *out of it* the roar of its own fall, catching up to what's already death and burning . . . A ghost in the sky." The virus is like this ghost in the sky, a silent passing. You don't know until afterward, once the coughing starts, the fever begins, exploding after you've already been hit, catching up to what's already death and burning. The rainbow is the pandemic's trajectory, the curve under which comes life or death.

The English statistician Roger Mexico and servicewoman

Jessica Swanlake lie awake under the threat of this rainbow, snuggled up in bed, their affair in hiding, hearing a rocket strike close by. Their hearts pound. Will the invisible death train spare them? Lying awake in bed, in quarantine, my wife and I have wondered likewise these past months, our hearts similarly pounding. Outside, the traffic stopped. We talked about the day's news—the bad news, the numbers, our fears, what will happen tomorrow, another day having passed. After a while, we stopped talking, just listened together in the silence.

From my bed comes an urge to run loose like Tyrone Slothrop, Pynchon's alter-ego anti-hero. The British and American military are running psychological tests on him in London, Pavlovian experiments. Yet he wrenches himself free from their grip and embarks on a search for himself and a rocket in the Zone—the ruins of Occupied Europe. It's 1944–1945, the war is officially over, yet battles still rage. In the Zone, reality isn't what it appears. There, a destructive military machine morphs into a destructive economic machine, squabbling over war spoils, trying to cash in on rocket technology. Industrial cartels (ICI, Shell, GE, Agfa, I.G. Farben) scramble for a piece of the peace.

Slothrop knows it's a scam, that sinister forces are orchestrating it all, out to get him, never coming clean. Today, we'd place the pharmaceutical, medical insurance, and techie cartels at the top of this roster of schemers. Plots get overlaid with counterplots, about which ordinary mortals have little inkling. Slothrop's right, of course, but the problem here is that reality follows one of his "Proverbs for Paranoids": "If they can get you asking the wrong questions, they don't have to worry about answers." Another problem seems to be our big problem: "There's nowhere to go, Slothrop," someone warns him, "nowhere." And it's true, a pandemic means literally that: it's everywhere, and we've no place to hide, not for long anyway, notwithstanding one's privileges.

The Zone unsettles in war's aftermath. Perhaps it is unsettling because, as we ease our lockdowns, it mirrors disarray and chaos. We bury the dead while convincing ourselves the worst is over. A crisis of truth-telling, a battlefield of unknowns and imponderables, of information blockage. Science versus anti-science, public health paling beside private gain, individual liberties stymying collective necessity. In our Zone, free-floating anguish prevails.

Slothrop chased the rainbow from point to point. Its arc reduced itself to a series of equations, to aerodynamics and electronics, to propulsion and insulation, to guidance systems. His quest was for a rocket —an "R"—with a serial number 00000, pointing northward. Epidemiology has its own "R" factor, pointing outward, exploding everywhere. This is the reproductive value of a virus, how infectious it is, the average number of people a single individual might infect with it. Our quest is for an R-0 or below (an R-negative), suggesting the virus's passage is diminishing. An R-value above 1 is bad since infection is spreading exponentially, being silently passed on to an ever-increasing number of persons.

Maybe Pynchon, our laureate of intrigue and paranoia, should write his next book about the pandemic, calling it *R*. After all, he's already written a *V.*, as well as a sort of V2, *Gravity's Rainbow*. Why not *R-Zero*, about a search for an epidemiological Holy Grail—a Coronavirus vaccine? An older rocket man Slothrop might engage in this latest mission, peeling back the investigative layers it'll likely necessitate, haunting the laboratories and corridors of institutional darkness. The novel might try to resolve the conundrum of our times: entropy, the measure of disorganization in a system, the collective chaos resulting from cosmic heat death. It might be a field guide to entropy management, offsetting our thermodynamical gloom, our own urban and social disintegration.

In the 1850s, German physicist Rudolf Clausius said the entropy of an isolated system always continually grew. Order and predictability gradually decline. In an early Pynchon story, "Entropy," from 1960, the character Callisto thought this an adequate metaphor to apply to our lot. "He was forced," Pynchon says, "in the sad dying fall of middle age, to a radical re-evaluation of everything he had learned up to then; all the cities and seasons and casual passions of his days had now to be looked at in a new and elusive light."

Callisto confronted entropy the same way Pynchon confronts it: by hermetically sealing himself off, constructing in his apartment a tiny enclave of regularity in the city's chaos. It's one mode to survive a pandemic; withdraw and avoid the crowd's heat and intensity. But it mightn't be the most resilient method to maintain healthy human relations. Perhaps the other solution is the alternative Pynchon touts in the final part of *Gravity's Rainbow*—a counterforce, a dialectical ballet of force meeting an opposition, a collision that establishes a new order, a new urban order—post-plague. "Creative paranoia," Pirate Prentice reminds Roger Mexico, "means developing at least as thorough a We-system as a They-system."

A counterforce is scattered throughout the Zone, even throughout our own Zone. It's there to disarm and dismantle the Man. Melvillians believe Ahab is the Man, the avatar of our times, the narcissist who eventually sinks his ship. Yet the masochistic Nazi rocket captain Blicero—"White Death"—seems more representative of our demented political incumbents, our "populists" who climax in tyranny and demagogy, in seeing giant penises launch into the sky, photo-shooting the countdown. As the rockets rain, falling at nearly a mile a second, there's still time, Pynchon says, if you need comfort, to touch the person next to you, that there is always a hand to turn the time. This thought

alone is enough to bring on a moment's soporific calm—before
another restless night . . .


I WROTE THE ABOVE RATHER cryptic piece on Thomas
Pynchon's *Gravity's Rainbow* in June 2020. I'd been reading
Pynchon's book for several months prior, when going out was
restricted and everybody was unsure about what was happening to our lives. Schools were closed, the death count was rising.
It was hard to grasp what had besieged us, what had destroyed
ordinary everyday life everywhere. Pynchon's narrative about a
rocket that killed people silently seemed terribly prescient for the
silent death striking many of us down. The sense of uncertainty,
the anxieties, the dramas and conspiracies—all were Pynchon's
terrain, his literary forte. Our poet laureate of paranoia had found
his latter-day muse.

Rereading this essay recently, I decided I wanted to adapt it
to launch this book. I wanted to begin my conversation about
post-plague urbanism with a memorandum about that plague,
about how it felt when it was raging, when we all had little inkling
of what lay ahead and who would drop next. Like a lot of past
plagues, it didn't seem picky: it was striking down all comers, the
healthy as well as the sickly. Literature helped me articulate that
unnerving feeling; reading *Gravity's Rainbow* was oddly comforting in an atmosphere of frightening discomfort.

Pynchon's rainbows are V-2 rocket arcs, the trajectory of mis-
siles that one hears only after it has exploded; if you heard it,
you were safe—for now. But rainbows also glow, signal where the
yellow brick road begins, where it is lit up. They're symbols of
hope in the distance: they stake out where the Zone ends and
the passage one must take to get there. The most exciting and
suggestive parts of Pynchon's book, the most mysterious and

compelling, focus on the Zone. *Beyond Plague Urbanism* is about the passage through this Zone, about the journey beyond it.

Our Zone is urban life in transition, our tundra on the edge, which, for a while, seemed like a no-man's land of desolation, an interstitial space of deserted streets and boarded-up stores; only those with no place else to go lurked in public, hung out on street corners, huddled in doorways. It was our Zone of unoccupied confinement, of shadowy menace, of waiting for the end of the world or maybe watching it already unfold. Maybe I was, at last, absorbing what Pynchon meant in *Gravity's Rainbow*: that in the Zone, "entropy management" had its work cut out, that we needed to measure the level of disorganization of our system, the social heat-death before us, here, now, not in 1944. Our own streets were full of thermodynamical gloom.

In Pynchon's early story, "Entropy," Callisto said that with entropy, "you can't win, things are going to get worse before they get better, [and] who says they're going to get better." Callisto was aged fifty-four, almost a decade younger than I am now, and forced to admit, "in the sad dying fall of middle-age," that everything needed "radical re-evaluation," that "all cities and seasons and casual passions of his days had now to be looked at in a new and elusive light." I had to nod in agreement. Perhaps things would never get better, and we had to manage and maximize what we already had, needed to cling onto it, make micro-good against a background of worsening macro-bad.

Are we seeing cities headed from a state of relative order toward a condition of increasing chaos? Can we talk of such a thing as *urban entropy*? Could life reach a point where, as Callisto thought, we'd "ultimately have the same quantity of energy; and all intellectual motion would, accordingly, cease." Maybe we've already reached that point? Maybe we're experiencing growing entropy where increasing disorder begets its paradoxical social analog: uniformity and conformity, less and less deviation and uniqueness? Is it the manifest destiny of cities everywhere to more or less function alike, to expend the same economic energy, to generate nothing culturally new, nothing novel or innovative, no new art, no new life forms, nothing productive? Are cities little more than commercial territories where wealth is fracked by the few at the expense of the many?

You can't escape the inevitability of entropy; Callisto knew it. Perhaps his neighbor downstairs in the Pynchon story, Meatball Mulligan, whose raucous "lease-breaking party" had entered its noisy fortieth hour, knew it too, as he tried to wind things down and get revelers to go home. The latter's beatnik blast, with drunken bodies randomly coming and going, its benzedrine and booze binges, its improvised jazz and people passing out, its chaos and communication overload, was a counterpoint to Callisto's closed system, to his climatically controlled enclave. No air circulated in one apartment; too much leaked into the other.

And yet, open or closed, neither avoided entropy. In the story's closing scene, Callisto's girlfriend, Aubade, breaks their apartment window, smashes it with her fists, letting the chaos of the outside flood in, recognizing that you can't escape the reality of this outside, can't avoid long-range heat-death, no matter what. Her "two exquisite hands came away bleeding and glistening with splinters," says Pynchon. Aubade knew that to start afresh, you had to take risks (remember, an *aubade* is an early morning hymn or poem, and, in French, *aube* means "dawn," the beginning of a new day). She knew that you can't run away or hide, can't live in an airless hyper-controlled void, sealed off from the world. You have to create friction and use friction creatively, embrace disorder as potentially productive, as something critical, necessary for incubating new culture, for encouraging new encounters and conversations, new arguments and engagements.

Conversations flow with a dramatic intensity at Meatball's party. Some are intimate; others rambling, the nonsense uttered under the influence. But all express an inter-subjectivity. At one point, Meatball talks to his friend Saul about "communication theory." Saul says all the conversations he hears are really "noise," something that "screws up your signal, makes for disorganization in the circuit." Meatball knows little about this, nothing about communication theory, yet he does know how to talk. He says that maybe Saul is asking too much of people. Making noise with words is what we do; it's a uniquely human act. Cities are where we all make the loudest noise, exchange lots of words. "I mean," says Meatball, "you know, what it is is, most of the things we say, I guess, are mostly noise." "Ha! Half of what you just said, for example" (Saul). "You never run at top efficiency," Meatball muses, "usually all you have is a minimum basis for a workable thing. I believe the phrase is 'Togetherness.'"

To converse is thus an act of human Togetherness, even in disagreement. The conversations taking place in this book try to affirm a certain human Togetherness. They attempt to communicate ideas and sentiments, stir up concerns, raise collective spirits. Not a few have been murmured as internal dialogues, as self-reflections, as conversations with myself. Other times they've been engagements with books and texts, when I've conversed with characters between the lines as one might converse with real people. Elsewhere, I do talk to real people, in person, to urbanists and practitioners, to scholars of cities and life. Meantime, because the specter of COVID surrounds so much of this book's writing, many conversations have also been carried out virtually over Zoom.

My most important conversations have always been with the city itself, with cities lost and found, old and new, real and imagined, traveled through and lived in. In this sense, I like to think of the city as a Great Book inspiring a liberal education, the kind that the American educational philosopher Robert Hutchins said teaches you how to become a citizen of the world. In the 1950s, Hutchins invoked "The Great Conversation." Maybe now we need to initiate "The Great Urban Conversation," resuscitate the city as a vast open-air public library, as a seat of learning where you receive lessons on humanism, on how to be a citizen with rights and responsibilities. Alas, these days, the city seems to have lost its collective way, turned anti-human: it has remaindered a lot of its classics and closed down public access, auctioning off its campus to the highest bidder. But we need to redraft this Great Book together, dialogue anew about its table of contents, re-type-setting the future social life contained within its leaves.

Will such a Great Urban Conversation turn out to be a quest for some *Invisible City*, the likes of which Italo Calvino described in his dialogue between Kublai Khan and Marco Polo? We'll have to see. Remember how Polo journeyed throughout Khan's Tartar empire, exploring its crystal cities. He recounts his urban adventures to an emperor who'd only ever dreamed about these exotic places, never seeing them for real. Khan had strolled around them often in his mind.

When the emperor tells Polo of his urban dreams, he asks whether they correspond to reality. The explorer says they do. But we can't be sure he's telling the truth. Perhaps he's just evoking his own fantasies since he's describing cities not located on any map. They're real yet fantastical places, composite yearnings. After a while, we realize that Khan and Polo mightn't be talking about real cities at all—at least none we recognize in bricks and mortar, in glass and steel. They're *ideas* about cities, thought experiments.

Later, Polo muses, saying he's only been trying to conceive the perfect city in his head, piece it together, bit by bit, fragment by fragment, forming a totality made of instances separated in time and space, a model city from which all cities can be deduced. At the end of their dialogue, he confesses to Khan: "If I tell you that the city toward which my journey tends is discontinuous in space and time, now scattered, now more condensed, you must not believe the search for it can stop."

2

OUR LIVELIEST CITIES ARE THOSE with the greatest diversity. Diversity of activities, diversity of people. Jane Jacobs long ago highlighted the link between economic diversity and social vitality; how the former fuels the latter, how economic activity ensures the presence of people, concentrations of people, different kinds of people, who in assorted ways help keep economic activity afloat.

Henri Lefebvre, in France, made pretty much the same point, if in a different register. He wasn't so much interested in the economic forces that create diversity as in how diversity creates dynamic *encounters*. Cities, for him, are sites of encounters, dense and differential social spaces in which people assemble. City spaces come alive through proximity, through concentrations of different social groups and activities, gathering in place. Lefebvre said the enemy of encounters, indeed the enemy of urbanization itself, is *segregation* and *separation*, two profoundly destructive impulses.

Over past decades, long before COVID, the diversity that Jacobs extols and the encounters animating Lefebvre's urban visions have withered, undergone their own entropy. Any urban dweller with their eyes and ears open will know that the form and function of our cities have been moving in the exact opposite direction. Jacobs emphasized the need for high and middling yield enterprises mingling with low and no-yield enterprises. Instead, predatory city economies have throttled small businesses: high yield has become the only asking price. Many corner stores and street corner people have been forced out of business and out of town. Cities have become functionally and financially standardized, predictable and unaffordable, predictably unaffordable, sucking dry their vitality, their Jacobean lifeblood.

And then COVID assailed us, upending urban life as we knew it, intensifying those already existing pathologies. Economic distancing had been gnawing away at the urban fabric for a while, executing the separation Lefebvre feared so much. Soon social distancing would break into urban densities, crimping cities as sites of physical encounters. Suddenly, our new urban reality is one of *de-encounter*, a thinning down rather than thickening up, the dispersion and dilution of city life, its fear and avoidance.

Same story the world over: a wealthy urban exodus, a hunkering down by the shore, up a hilltop, at the country estate, anywhere without people. As the pandemic raged, the rich who'd been colonizing citadels everywhere, shaping them in their own crass class image, exited fast. Between March 1 and May 1, 2020, the first two months of lockdown, 420,000 of New York's wealthiest quit town, Manhattan's Upper East Side emptied out by 40 percent. Denizens fled to second homes upstate, in Long Island, Connecticut, and Florida. "Farewell Poor People," said the *Daily Mail*, catching the spirit of London's select out-migration. Its most well-heeled populations similarly headed for rural sanctuary, paying up to £50,000 per month in rentals. British estate agents have since been inundated with requests for country mansions and isolated manor houses.

In times of plague, the rich outrunning the spread of infection has been a time-honored tactic. In *A Journal of the Plague Year* (1722), Daniel Defoe describes the harrowing scenes of the 1665 "*Poors Plague*," the bubonic epidemic that struck London, striking it unevenly. The famed author of *Robinson Crusoe* narrates his tale of the Great Plague through the lens of an alter-ego character, an independent merchant, H.F., who'd agonized about whether to stay or flee London like his class peers. Eventually, unlike them, he decides to stay put, ventures out, walks the streets, and bears witness to the mass slaughter of a terrifying disease few understood.

In 1665, Defoe would have been a five-year-old lad, so *A Journal of the Plague Year* is a novelistic invention—an artistic creation based on historical fact. Like the good journalist he was, Defoe did his research thoroughly, read meticulously around the plague, the books, pamphlets, and scientific studies. H.F. evokes graphic details reliably accurate and believable from the standpoint of an authentic observer: the desolate streets and parishes, the shut-up shops, the overrun cemeteries, the fevers and vomiting, the pains and swellings, the destruction of whole families, and the reality of 97,000 Londoners perishing because of a bacillus now known to be a parasite of rodents, transported by fleas.

H.F. is a sympathetic, if eccentric, *flâneur*, both fascinated and frightened by the disease, compassionate about the calamities afflicting populations that bore its brunt, that suffered the greatest death toll. He shares something of his creator's philosophy of life, that love and mercy, not fear, brought people to salvation. (One of Defoe's chief purposes in writing *A Journal of the Plague Year* was to lobby for improved public administration during plagues.) Even the poor's insurrectional tendencies found a considerate ear. At one point, H.F. distinguishes between "good" and "bad" mobs, between dissenting peoples whose marauding cause seemed legitimate, and those who seemed to be acting because they were deluded by false propaganda.

Some people were "really overcome with Delusions," says

Freedom /Responsibility

H.F. (the curious uppercases throughout *A Journal* are Defoe's own), propagated by con men peddling quack remedies, spreading fallacious rumors that filled people's "Heads with Predictions and Signs of the Heavens." It strikes an oddly contemporary chord, anticipating our own COVID crisis moment. Con men here have similarly promised quack remedies (one using bleach!). Economic inequities are ripping our society apart, crosscut by intensely waged ideological battles—between mask-wearers and right-wing anti-maskers, between "Black Lives Matter" protesters and White Supremacists. (Subsequent debates about vaccination rollouts have further widened these cleavages.) Separation and segregation now encounter one another. Our public life has fractured into trench civil warfare; a tense political and cultural standoff defines the public realm even more direly than it did in Defoe's day.

Public space is a menace, a threat to public health, not only because of the spread of virus but also because it is fraught with institutional and popular violence: "*I can't breathe*" is one expression of the former, immortalizing George Floyd's dying words on a Minneapolis street, as a white cop pressed his knee into the black man's neck. "*Don't shoot!*" is another, after Michael Brown's valedictory plea in Ferguson, Missouri, before the police opened fire, heralding a spate of police killings of young, unarmed black men (and women), on the street and sometimes in the home.

Right-wing libertarians say forcing people to wear face masks in public is an assault on individual freedom, an infringement of personal liberty. It's another instance that unfettered self-interest is best; that a greedy drive for profit maximization and unregulated consumer choice brings about a healthier, more robust society. It doesn't. It's a foil for selfishness that bears no responsibility for how it hurts others, economically or otherwise. The mask isn't only personal protective equipment: it's there to ensure other people's health isn't put at risk. There have to be limits to what is deemed acceptable individual behavior in public, accepting the fact that forcing people to wear masks also raises questions of democracy. There's more need than ever for a just social contract, for a democratic covenant in which everybody recognizes shared duties and individual rights.

It's a touchy subject. Yet it's an agenda Jean-Jacques Rousseau set himself over two and a half centuries ago, forty years after Defoe's *Journal*, and its basis remains instructive about what we still lack: "a form of association that defends and protects the person and goods of each with the common force of all." "I had seen that everything is rooted in politics," Rousseau said, "and that, whatever the circumstances, a people will never be other than the nature of its government makes it." "Great questions as to which is the best possible form of government," he thought, "seems to me to come down in the end to this one: what is the nature of the government most likely to produce the most virtuous, the most enlightened, the wisest, and in short, taking this word in its widest sense, the best people?"

It's a tall order to conceive of people as virtuous, enlightened, and wise. As presidents and prime ministers bully, lie, and peddle misinformation, stoke up hatred and division within society, they've rendered us stupid. They've destroyed our collective ability to judge truth from falsehood, good sense from (social) media nonsense. Some describe this as a denigration of "cognitive immunity," the destruction of our mental defense system, the ability to ward off pathological ideas, just as our immune system might ward off a pathological disease. We have what we deserve: an *anti-social contract*, a model of government hoodwinking its populace into believing it is free, that it is upholding individual liberty when, in actuality, our minds have become enslaved.

PAST PANDEMICS—FROM PLAGUE in Ancient Greece and the
Roman Empire's Plague of Justinian to Europe's bubonic epidem-
ics in the Middle Ages and eighteenth century, passing through
typhoid and cholera outbreaks in the nineteenth, onwards to
"Spanish flu" in 1918 and the latest COVID epidemic—all reveal
underlying crises in their societies. Plagues sparked tragedy yet
were often *outcomes* of crises, not initial causes, a symptom of
something lurking within the culture, about to give, a growing
malaise, soon to worsen.

COVID is no different, exposing structural defects in our
economy and politics, in our encroachment into the natural
world, our destruction of it; and how zoonotic diseases like
COVID now more virulently jump from animals to humans.
After it had jumped all over us, our mix of underfunded public
and for-profit private healthcare systems proved woefully inad-
equate to cope. The virus spread like the wildfire and flash-flood-
ing ever more frequent in our midst. Another hurricane hit, and
our urban system took a pounding.

Maybe history is on our side, expressive of long-wave good
news. Or is it? Have we reached limits? Has some kind of entro-
pic condition gripped us? Does it preclude recovery, trap us in
a state of permanent limbo, an eternal present that holds no real
future? Humans have, up until now at least, survived tragedy and
disappointment through incredible stoicism and creativity. Wars,
plagues, and mass ransacking of cities in Ancient Greece gave
us poetry like *The Iliad*, epic drama like *Trojan Women*, schol-
arship like Thucydides's *History of the Peloponnesian War*, and
Plato's *Republic*.

Black Death ravaged Florence in 1348, shook up Italian
society, killed thousands; yet it produced Boccaccio's bawdy
masterpiece *The Decameron* and the wide-ranging social, economic, cultural, and religious changes that eventually led to

the Renaissance, history's greatest epoch for art, architecture, and literature. When bubonic plague devastated seventeenth-century Britain, theaters closed, and Shakespeare's plays could no longer be performed. But none of this prevented our bard from writing them, from letting his creative juices flow in the misery and isolation, penning such masterpieces as *King Lear*, *Macbeth*, and *Antony and Cleopatra*.

In the mid-1850s, Marx lived through a cholera epidemic in London's Soho that killed hundreds of people because of a contaminated water pump. He was destitute, had several children die before him, and was lodged in a dreadful apartment. Economic crisis deepened, workers' revolt dissipated. All the same, Marx continued to work throughout, never stopped studying capitalism, never let up writing *Das Kapital*. He never stopped hoping, telling his comrade Friedrich Engels that "in all the terrible agonies I have experienced these days, the thought of you and your friendship has always sustained me, and the hope that, together, we may still do something sensible in the world."

In the twentieth century, disgust with an economic and political order that plunged us into two murderous world wars helped spark Surrealism, a revolutionary movement that affirmed its extraordinarily creative dialectic. On the one hand, came Max Ernst's brilliant pictorial horror story, "After the Rain II," painted

between 1940–1942, a hellscape of hope smothered by petrified and calcified structures, by corpses and decayed vegetation, by deformed creatures in a prehistoric premonition of our own COVID fate.  ⌐ WWⅡ ⌐

On the other hand emerged an optimism, art and literature that celebrated the dawn of romantic love, that primal form of Surrealist encounter, epitomized by André Breton's *Mad Love*. As fascist bombs rained on Guernica and Hitler's Third Reich was about to stomp across Europe, Breton wrote: "I have never ceased to believe that, among all the states through which humans can pass, love is the greatest supplier of solutions, being at the same time in itself the ideal place for the joining and fusion of these solutions." (Three decades on, John Coltrane's *A Love Supreme* nodded in agreement. As racial hatred raged across America, its triumphant choruses sought "resolution" through love.)

Breton closed *Mad Love* with a touching letter to baby daughter Aube, addressing her as a future sixteen-year-old, as a teenager tempted to open her father's old book, whose title, he hoped, "will be wafted to you euphonically by the wind bending the hawthorns." "Whatever will be your lot," dad said, "increasingly fortunate or entirely other, I cannot know, you will delight in living, expecting everything from love." "I WANT YOU TO BE MADLY LOVED," Breton said, in his great rally-crying gift to posterity, to future generations. What will we have to show for our post-COVID Renaissance I wonder?

Perhaps what we're experiencing now is an interregnum that progressives need to ride out, need to struggle through, sustain ourselves by hope, by a love supreme, by friendship, believing there's light somewhere beyond the gloom, some way still to do something sensible in the world. This, too, will pass. Hopefully. Then again, maybe it won't. Maybe we can only try again, fail better. Perhaps we can use what time is left to reflect together on how we might reconstruct the public realm of our cities, even the public realm of our lives.

We can plot another public world, do it together, from the underground, where dissidents and activists have traditionally hidden out when the political going has been rough. We might even reframe the notion of "intimacy," develop online links with others, collapse social distancing on the outside through time-space compression on the inside, via our computer screens, via the Zoom communities that continue to sprout. With Zoom, not only can we look at people's faces, but we can also enter their homes, personal spaces, see the art on the wall, the books on the bookshelves, the family photos. Zoom lets us share a strange, often enlarged sociability and camaraderie, permitting gatherings of people that literally stretch across the globe. It captures vaster and more diverse audiences than we could ever imagine in one place, face-to-face. It's not the same as face-to-face encountering, but let's use it to find nourishment in this interregnum, share ideas, launch discussion and reading groups, webinars, and virtual gatherings. Let's talk and debate and listen to one another, organize one another, forge solidarity in kind, preceding it in person.

Some conversations have already begun to probe what post-pandemic cities might do to bounce back. The key theme seems to be ushering fresh air into urban life, creating cities that flourish in the open, as al fresco playhouses. We need to bring a touch of Ancient Greece back into our civilization, where open-air amphitheaters became scenes of political and intellectual communion. Research indicates that we're twenty times more likely to catch COVID indoors than outdoors. There's a need to reimagine a different open-air public life, more resilient to future pandemics, with different spaces and places, accessible spaces and places—developing commercial and recreational activities that not only entice people back into cities but offer enough to make people want to stay, feel safe as well as stimulated.

Design initiatives propose squeezing roads to widen pedestrian sidewalks and enlarging café and restaurant terraces; radiant heating and cooling technology can extend outdoor seasonal usages. Future cities will be a lot greener, more walkable and bikeable. Cars and car-oriented infrastructure will get scaled back. Abandoned lots and obsolete multistory car parks might flourish as urban farms, using hydroponics, providing cheaper, fresher produce for neighborhoods on their doorsteps, minimizing food miles and distribution costs. Such innovations now seem *de rigueur*, standard repertoires in design game plans. Ditto opening up streets and parkland to vendors and commercial activity, reanimating open-air city retailing, allowing it to be improvised and spontaneous—maybe like it once was.

After decades of "quality of life" campaigns, this would be an enormous volte-face for a city like New York. Since the mid-1990s, during Giuliani's mayoral years, Business Improvement Districts have waged war on unlicensed street activities, converting Manhattan into a glorified corporate suburban theme park, funneling people into the chain malls, cleansing the streets of grubby diversity—of food stands and street peddlers, of artists and homeless booksellers, stuff that brought vitality to many sidewalks.

Al fresco city life has always thrilled our most romantic urbanists. Romantic urbanists sat in cafés, wrote books, fretted home alone, but their real muse was without a roof, amid the crowd, out on the sidewalk—no matter the weather. It was an open-air intimacy among strangers. The poet Charles Baudelaire wanted us to embrace the crowd, to bathe in the multitude, take universal communion. He said we might find ourselves as we get lost in public, as we merge with the masses, though not too close.

André Breton said his great heroine, Nadja, enjoyed being nowhere but in the street. *Nadja* is one of the strangest romances ever written, locating itself in that liminal zone where dream and reality blur, where we're left wondering if any of this tale really happened—this infatuation with a woman, this infatuation with the streets of Paris. Nadja, the phantom woman who'd chosen for herself the name "Nadja," because in Russian it marked the beginning of the word *hope* and because she, Nadja, was only a beginning. In the street, one gray fall afternoon, Nadja and André first lay eyes on each other. She smiled "quite mysteriously," Breton says, "and somehow *knowingly*." (His italics.) He "asked her one question which sums up all the rest, a question only I, probably, would ever ask, but which has at least once found a reply worthy of it: 'who are you?' And she, without a moment's hesitation: 'I am the wandering soul.'"

Street encounters like these were *modern* encounters. They symbolized what the Surrealists called the "new spirit," a thoroughly urban spirit, where people, by chance, "freely" encountered one another out in the public realm; never, certainly, on equal terms, but the gaze would cut both ways, could look back. People watched one another, lost and found one another, and did so amid the throng. It was the stuff of modern poetry as well as modern city life.

Jane Jacobs said the best streets have the most dynamic choreographies—"intricate street ballets"—changing with the time of day, never repeating themselves from place to place. We've seen some of these choreographies adapt and change during the pandemic, as dancers dodge and sway, twirl with other members of the ensemble, guarding social distance on city streets everywhere. But Jacobs knew that sidewalks needed more than just urban design to keep them alive. We need a bolder vision of how to reintroduce public life and make it exciting and romantic again.

*Buy local*

Local commerce, for a start, needs life support even more than in pre-COVID times. Twenty-one thousand British small businesses went under during March's 2020 lockdown. The British Chamber of Commerce fears as many as one million little enterprises might eventually collapse, leaving empty shells and permanently boarded up main streets across the land. New York lost three thousand small businesses during its March quarantine. Many Manhattan street corners are boarded up and graffiti splattered. Big retail chains have made conscious choices to elope. After years of plundering, seeing off little independent competitors, sucking the life out of many New York blocks, big brands like Gap, JCPenney, Subway, and Domino's Pizza led the charge out.

In our largest cities, common wealth has been squandered by conspicuously wasteful large enterprises administered by elites who thrive off unproductive activities: they roll the dice on the stock market, dance to shareholder delight, profit from unequal exchanges, guzzle at the public trough, filch rents and treat land

and property as a pure financial asset. Invariably, too, they dodge their tax burden. They leech blood money out of urban territories, underwriting what might be termed "parasitic city" development, antithetical to the "generative city" that any public action plan would now need to reinitiate.

City life has to avoid a Hobbesian war of all against all where the deck is rigged, stacked against little businesses as well as little people. Some commercial rent and business rate control is required. When urban economies thrive, commercial landlords hike rents, speculate and inflate property markets, and become the "monstrous power" that Marx recognized. "One section of society," Marx said, "demands a tribute from the other for the right to inhabit the earth." In downturns, when the economy dips, landlords prefer to sit on vacant property, leave premises empty until they find tenants able to pay the market rent, the inflated market rent. It's a double whammy that inevitably works both ways against less resourceful tenants.

A carrot option for municipalities is to offer landlords tax incentives to release commercial space at more affordable rents, making it worthwhile to see rents reduced. Yet there are harder alternatives, too, bolder policies that might be pursued, which necessitate a stick. One could be the creation of a "living rent" program, a landed counterpart to the living wage ordinances already passed in many cities worldwide. A living rent would be a rent that enables small business owners to earn a living, to pay for a lease in accordance with their modest income streams.

In a property market designed *not* to rip people off, potential small business concepts might become real practical endeavors; little entrepreneurs are encouraged to take the risk, to go for it. A living rent would allow landlords to receive a rent-controlled return, a fair return, not an extortionate, parasitic return, subject to taxation at an appropriate rate. Leases would be negotiated

"N FAIR return"

over five-year terms. At each renewal, living rents would be reca-
librated according to the tenant's past and prospective future
earnings. Refusal of landlords to comply with living rent ordinances would mean that the municipality sequesters the property
and procures it as a public landlord.

Imagine how small generative activities might flourish in such
an incubating culture. By themselves, they'd be modest ventures.
But scattered around a whole city, they'd collectively add up to
a lot. They'd signal the return of the re-skilled worker in the city,
empowered in their labor process, answerable to themselves and
their locale. These artisans would pioneer little start-ups, offer
training programs around the re-skilling of old skills, the likes
of which we'd already begun to glimpse pre-COVID. In grungy,
abandoned areas of town, we've seen micro-breweries and dis-
tilleries prosper in small-scale fabrication units. Let's hope they
continue to prosper, and have other artisanal activities emerge
alongside, post-COVID: bakers and candlestick makers, book-
binders and printers, potters and carpenters, furniture repairers
and cheesemakers, welders and sculptors, clothes and craft producers, artists and urban farmers. We can imagine them together,
bringing a little diversity and curiosity back into neighborhoods,
doing so without sparking gentrification, kept at bay through
commercial rent control. Small artisanal producers are usually
satisficers, not profit maximizers. They become the latter only in a
commercial environment that compels them to become the latter,
that forces upon them that bitter taste of capitalist "success."

Meantime, city officials need to think hard about what they
will do with the glut of office space that remote work now beto-
kens, the new norm for the privileged white-collar employee.
Much of this office space was speculatively built, produced by
over-accumulated capital, and colossally unnecessary even at the
best of times. Now, at the worst of times, we have it looming large,

like a dark cloud over urban space. It's a lesson in how to kill a
city, to make large swaths dull, the kind of dullness only money
can buy, despite its glitz.

But here, again, imagine how vast open-planned floors could
be rezoned and converted into affordable individual dwellings
and family homes, with real space between partition walls, fitted
out with balconies and breathable outdoor terraces. City governments could obtain the leases or the freeholds of these premises, recruit local architectural practices to engage in innovative
designs; local construction companies (supported by unions
flush with cash) might undertake the actual rehab itself.

City ownership

Importantly, some of this affordable housing would need to be
set aside for younger people. Since lockdown, millennials have
undertaken a mass urban exodus, and this flight continues everywhere, from New York and London to Paris and Tokyo, and lots
of big cities in between. Even before COVID, younger people
were wilting under the pressure of exorbitant big-city costs. They
endured tiny domestic spaces because of the wealth of ameni-
ties outside, on their doorstep—bars and restaurants, theaters
and art galleries, cultural attractions, the sheer energy of flocks
of people, the sense of opportunity. But when these attractions
closed and streets were shorn of people, costly big cities quickly
lost their luster. Their bright lights have dimmed. We're still not
sure about any future illumination. Many millennials opted for
cheaper small towns; others work remotely from their parents'
homes. All wonder if they'll ever return to city life again.

It says a lot about our civilization, about what's gone wrong,
when young people flee too expensive cities. The high cost is no
longer worth the hassle. The city's promise has been a letdown. It
bodes badly for our urban future, a loss of young creative capacity, leaving a worrying urban footprint in their stead. Historically,
cities were places where young people always flocked, went there

to liberate themselves, to grow up in public, as independent adults, beyond their parents' grasp. The city was an existential rite of passage. As the cost of living soars, the city's romance is already talking alimony.

Anybody who has ever watched French *nouvelle vague* cinema, directed by the likes of Jean-Luc Godard, François Truffaut, and Louis Malle, will have felt this urban romance, imbibed its moody atmosphere. Much of the dialogue and action in these films unfolds in the street, in the everyday public realm, on a café terrace, up and down the boulevard, 24/7. The city is where young people fell in and out of love, argued about politics, read books, wrote books, discovered themselves, extended themselves. In cities, you broadened your horizons, deepened your whole being.

Malle's enchanting film of Raymond Queneau's enchanting book, *Zazie dans le Métro*, is remarkable at showing the wide-eyed fascination cities hold (held?) for young people. The protagonist Zazie is a sharp-tongued kid from the provinces, let loose in Paris, spending the weekend with Uncle Gabriel, the oddball brother of her mother who dances dressed as a woman in a seedy nightclub. By day, Gabriel tries to show Zazie the famous sights of his native city, but he's always muddling up their names, and she's not interested in them anyway, not in any tourist city. Nor is he, really. "I don't give a shit about that," Zazie tells him, using her trademark *gros mots*. "What are you interested in then?" asks Uncle Gaby. "The Métro," says Zazie. That's the source of her fascination: people, crowds, and liberty. But that weekend, a transport workers' strike means the Métro is closed. She throws a tantrum, curses her luck, and flees to explore the streets on her own, causing mayhem wherever she goes, encountering all sorts of quirky and shady characters. At the story's close, when she's reunited with her mother, the latter wonders whether Zazie has had a good time. "*Comme ça,*" says Zazie. "*J'ai vieilli,*" she says—she's aged, grown up, learned a few things.

Few young people ever went to live in cities to earn lots of money. Indeed, cities were places where the young preferred to be poor because there you led a richly adventurous life, there you grew up. Almost instinctively, you engaged with the city as a Great Book. The city was more than a moneyman's spreadsheet, a map of real estate values, like it is today; more than a technocrat's algorithm where "expert" professionals and business types reimagine "Smart Cities," counting and classifying everything, digitally gathering information, amassing Big Data to create cities as seamless webs of connectivity, as the "Internet of Things," factoring out any of Jacobs's messiness, any richly adventurous life, anything Queneau's Zazie ever yearned for. Instead, they promise a brave new "Science of Cities," a mesh of objects and entities, interwoven in a smooth, frictionless space where people and information flow and commerce flourishes.

It's a frighteningly banal prospect, like an afternoon in a giant, paperless Apple store. "There's a feeling about that cause-and-effect may have been taken as far as it will go," Roger Mexico grumbles in *Gravity's Rainbow*. "That for science to carry on at all, it must look for a less narrow, less sterile set of assumptions. The next great breakthrough may come when we have the courage to junk cause-and-effect entirely and strike off at some new angle." The Great Urban Conversation similarly needs to strike off at some new angle, to start up another dialogue about the city as a start-up, a new urbanism of encounter.

Can we find the civic leadership courageous enough, visionary and intelligent enough, to step up to the plate, to accept this challenge and help us discover a new public action plan, a new social contract, making our minds and cities generative again? It's hard to tell. Some days it seems impossible. Yet despite the

*Vi 'scientific' sterility*

gloom, I can't quite give up the ghost, can't quite give up hope for
a future beyond COVID, beyond what we have now, beyond the
Trumps, Johnsons, and Putins, beyond a world as a dread Zone.
I can't quite give up hope for an urbanism that might one day
inspire rather than plague us.

*the Dread*
*zone —*
*(Title)*

3

NOT LONG AGO, I WAS IN SEOUL—well, sort of. I'd been there
before, for real, five years back. This time I was invited to talk
at the Seoul Urban Regeneration International Conference, with
its inflection on post-COVID-19 cityscapes. World Bank and
UN-Habitat bigwigs, together with academic planning experts,
were all present, rapping away virtually. My own online stint was
an annex panel called "Special Talk," tagged on at the end of
the two-day meeting, and it comprised a conversation between
myself, Hakjin Kim, Seoul's Vice-Mayor, Soontak Suh, the president of the University of Seoul, and Mike Batty, from London's
Bartlett School of Planning.

Seoul itself, a metropolis of ten million people, figured high
on the conference agenda: what challenges does COVID throw
up for the city's economic base? What are the new infrastruc-
tural requirements for mega-cities like Seoul? How does social
distancing affect community solidarity when face-to-face interaction is threatened? Mr. Kim, the city's Vice-Mayor, said Seoul
now faces enormous problems, but equally, he stressed, there are
new opportunities. A deeper question voiced was one I want to
elaborate on here: what kind of *values* should urban governance
embrace? Seoul's leaders were "seeking advice about which
direction to take urban regeneration."

I said that, coming from the United Kingdom, I felt uneasy

about giving advice to a country that has handled COVID so
ably. After all, former prime minister Boris Johnson blustered and
blundered his way through the COVID crisis, handling it awfully,
the worst of all Western nations, in terms of per capita death rates,
even worse than the United States. So there was little I could tell,
wanted to tell, South Korea, whose first confirmed case was on
January 24, 2020, and since then hasn't had any major lockdown.
Meantime, Britain's death toll has soared beyond one hundred
thousand, whereas South Korea's has barely nudged above six
thousand. This has had nothing to do with South Korea being
small; it isn't. It's a large country, with a population of around 51
million. Nor is it low-density. As of 2018, South Korea had 515
people per square kilometer, compared to the United Kingdom's
281 and England's 432. Seoul's density is 15,900 per square
kilometer, compared with 7,700 for London. (One square kilometer equals .039 square miles.)

South Korea's densely urbanized society has been incredibly
effective at suppressing COVID outbreaks. They've employed
excellent contract tracing and vigorous mass testing. Maybe most
vitally is that its people have unanimously complied with social
distancing rules. I said none of this surprised me, given what I'd
seen on my past visit to Seoul, one balmy spring week attending a conference. I told Mr. Kim and Mr. Suh that I remember
wandering around the city, looking and listening, mindful of Jane
Jacobs's dictum that urbanists "need an observant eye, curiosity about people, and a willingness to walk." Strolling through
Seoul's neighborhoods, I was struck by the city's quietness,
notwithstanding its magnitude and busyness, by its residents'
peacefulness, how dignified their interactions were with one
another in the public realm, in narrow streets and ubiquitous
little stores. There was a serenity and mutual respect you rarely
saw in Western cities anymore.

Seoul

In such a city, I said, mask-wearing probably wouldn't be an issue. People would doubtless don a mask in public because they know they have responsibilities toward others. Public space isn't just about *them*; it's a shared experience. Seoul's citizens seemed to understand implicitly what a social contract meant. Thus, if I had anything to say about Seoul, and South Korea, it would be that they had to defend this dignity in public, this *dignity of the public*, guard it as a badge of honor. They must continue to affirm the *value of the public realm*, keep it robust and healthy, because where I come from, it had been denigrated and torn apart.

Mr. Kim had his own take on this observation. He explained why he thought Korean society was less resistant to mask-wearing. A lot had to do with the city's rapid development, he said, how, since the 1960s, after the Korean War, its population increased two-fold every decade. Thirty years ago, the city had no systematic sewerage facility. Mr. Kim, who was around forty, remembers electricity arriving in his household when he was fifteen. It was then he also got his first pair of sneakers. Hitherto, he'd been walking around in rubber slippers, he said. He, like other people, still retained the memory of backwardness, a dark age nobody wanted to return to, a life without electricity and sneakers. If we didn't work together, he said, the COVID pandemic would shut us down, destroy our economic well-being, and propel us backward rather than forward.

I was glad Koreans remember their past because, I said, in Britain, people have forgotten. In the 1980s, throughout my twenties, Margaret Thatcher assumed the mantle of power and famously announced there was no such thing as society, "only individuals and families." It was the beginning of an ideology of possessive individualism, of a fervent, obsessive inculcation that the public sector was the problem and the private sector the solution. The public sector needed negating, right-wing pundits and ideologues insisted, replaced by free-market entrepreneurialism. New business paradigms would henceforth devise methods to deliver public services at minimum cost. Health and municipal services would be contracted out to low-balling private sector bidders; entire government departments were dissolved or replaced by new middle-management units whose machinations became as publicly transparent as mud.

Successive generations have been force-fed this ideology. Anything public is treated with suspicion, as shoddy and inefficient, as a third-class entity, something to be avoided. Only losers travel by mass transit when winners drive a car, frequently a big one, frequently many big ones; only the most vulnerable rent property, when the successful owner-occupy. All of this no longer appears ideological: it is embedded in people's brains as an objective reality, as it has always been. It's a belief system v McKinsey

that has taught people how to forget, how to turn their backs on the public realm and, ergo, on any social contract. Perhaps for good reason: the public state has been hollowed out to such a degree that it *is* shoddy. It seems perfectly natural nowadays to see public sector core functions—planning and the organization of services—outsourced to private consultants and contractors.

As the pandemic raged, the UK government had neither the hardware capacity nor the software know-how to deal with a massive *societal* problem. Instead, it doled out millions to "expert" consulting firms like McKinsey, which apparently did. When the latter instigated a National Health Service (NHS) test and trace system that hardly worked, we realized they, too, were clueless. (They were clueless in France, too, where McKinsey repeated its test and trace bungling.) Indeed, McKinsey is clueless and bungling about a lot of things, yet despite their serial cock-ups globally, including its deadly hand in the U.S. opioid crisis, they continue to get recruited and rake it in.

COVID exposed the shortcomings of the privatized state, the incompetence of private enterprise in addressing public health, and how public health challenges aren't resolvable by individuals and families alone. Mr. Kim was right to stress the importance of sneakers as cultural items for young people; but when a society prioritizes buying sneakers above everything else, like in the United Kingdom, affirming consumer sovereignty by the box load, we know then it has lost its collective way.

MR. SUH, THE UNIVERSITY of Seoul's president, seemed to know his Rousseau. He'd recognized I was alluding to the eighteenth-century author of *The Social Contract*, whose democracy defined freedom as *a recognition of collective necessity*. There's plenty of collective necessity involved in dealing

Rousseau

with a global pandemic and in dealing with a city during one. But collective necessity can only work if people recognize the state as "democratic" and know good government from bad. In populist nations like the United Kingdom and United States, democracy seems like a vision from another planet. We might call these *uncivil states* because people have lost their sense of duty to one another. They've been kidded by demagogues into thinking they're free agents capable of doing what they like, and if they can't, it's somebody else's fault. *They're* stopping *me* from doing something. Private inclinations have run roughshod over public interests.

But in Rousseau's civil state, a different morality would prevail. Rather than pursue narrow self-interests, people would "act according to other principles, and consult reason before heeding to inclination . . . their faculties are exercised and developed, their ideas expanded, their feelings ennobled, their entire soul soars so high . . . and out of a stupid, limited animal emerges an intelligent being." Somewhere inside us, an intelligent being lurks, yearning to burst out, someone who reaches out, upward, toward Rousseau's high bar, knowing that we've so far set this bar pathetically low. Intelligent creatures might acknowledge *society* again, that there is such a thing after all, that we can be freer if each of us admits we're part of a public culture that requires collective rebuilding.

Seoul's leaders shouldn't only defend public culture, I said, but post-COVID, they'll have to bring it to bear on private culture—on market culture. The social contract imposes limits not only on individual anti-social behavior; it equally reins in anti-social organizational behavior—the behavior of big businesses concerned only with big business. There are small businesses that serve local needs, that contribute to the public good; there are big businesses that serve shareholder greed, frequently *big v small business* (handwritten)

*This* (handwritten marginal note)

detrimental to this public good. (Of course, there are plenty of small businesses that rip off their workers, too, including their own family members; this likewise would be unacceptable under any just social contract.) Defending public interests is destined to disgruntle certain private interests, large and small, and doing so will require courageous leadership, honest leadership, the sort of civic leadership currently in short supply.

But demagogy destabilizes good leadership and undermines public culture. In the United Kingdom and United States, we've seen demagogy thrive. Politicians in both countries have freely engaged in what Jonathan Swift, half a century before Rousseau's *Social Contract*, labeled "the art of political lying." (Swift's essay appeared the year of Rousseau's birth, 1712.) The famed author of *Gulliver's Travels* said that even the stupidest lie has only to be believed for an hour for its work to be done. In our age, Twitter helps a lot. "Falsehood flies," lamented Swift, whereas "truth comes limping after it."

Salutary falsehoods no longer seem to disgruntle masses of people, let alone harm a demagogue's political career. On the contrary, they apparently assure this career, guarantee it, because there's a popular willingness to believe in falsehoods. Even when everybody knew Brexit would never save Britain's NHS £350 million a year, as Boris Johnson had bragged, or that Donald Trump was ever going to make America great again, the lie nonetheless became the necessary mood music for huge numbers of people. They wanted to hear it, *felt* the need to believe, to trust in its message. And 71 million Americans still do, insisting that Trump can still make their country great, and that the election was rigged.

Demagogy, from the ancient Greek word "demagoguery," initially had neutral and sometimes positive connotations. It meant simply "leading the *demos*," the Greek popular masses, the bulk of the people, the poorest if largest political class. One of the earliest deployments of demagoguery was in Aristophanes's comic drama *Knights*, publicly unveiled in 424 BC, to great acclaim. Pericles had died five years earlier, and Athens was still soul-searching for a worthy replacement. *Knights* captures the spirit of this leadership vacuum and the role of demagogy in the power struggle.

"Hard not to be outspoken/ When your political system's broken," the chorus of *Knights* bawls. Aristophanes's brilliance was to twist the meaning of demagogy, exposing it in its negative sense. The great playwright had seen how wannabe leaders mobilized rhetoric to manipulate the masses, seducing crowds for their own cynical, unscrupulous ends. "Demagoguery," Aristophanes had his character Demosthenes say, "no longer belongs to a man acquainted with / the things of the Muses or to one whose ways are upright, / But to one who is unlearned and loathsome."   dumb & slum

Cleon was the Donald Trump of Aristophanes's day, an arch-demagogue who flattered the people while secretly despising them, shamelessly slandering his enemies, taking bribes, lying, and manipulating the legal system—a West Wing playbook *avant la lettre*, using every ruse imaginable to retain power and accumulate wealth. Aristophanes had it in for demagogues like Cleon and the gullible Athenian demos that let the wool get pulled over its eyes, all-too-readily believing in the demagogue's hollow pledges. As Athenian citizens watched Aristophanes's drama, they found themselves implicated in the plot, often bearing the brunt of his jokes, lampooning and pillorying. They were laughing at themselves, and this, for Aristophanes, was the crux of political theater: the shock of recognition.

The unlikely hero of Aristophanes's *Knights* is a sausage-seller, a wizened streetwise old man. He pushes his portable kitchen into the agora, starts frying, and soon confronts Paphlagon—"the blusterer"—Cleon's theatrical stand-in. In front of them both is the demos, whom Aristophanes symbolizes as a single Athenian household, and a "chorus" of wealthy Athenians, the said "knights," riding on horseback. Paphlagon and the sausage-seller hurl abuse at one another. Their verbal combat, full of vulgarity and vaudeville, quickly takes on the tone of the theater of the absurd. The cunning street vendor, though uneducated, has been around the block a few times and raised in the "university of hard knocks"; he's a maestro of ironic putdown. And after a while, it is clear to everybody listening that the demagogue has met his match. He's exposed as the liar and charlatan he really is.

"How could there be a citizen, O Demos," Paphlagon proclaims, "who feels more / friendship for you than I do?" But the sausage-seller doesn't buy this tosh, responding: "he's the bloodiest bastard, O dearest little Demos, who's done the / crookedest misdeeds! / When you stand agape, / He breaks off the stalks of officials undergoing an audit / And gulps them down, and with both hands / He sops his bread in the public funds!" "I'll teach this very thing to you first," says the sausage-seller to the demos, "that he isn't your friend or well disposed, / . . . he gives no thought to you seated here on such hard rocks." "Why don't you judge, Demos, which of the two of us / Is the better man when it comes to you and your stomach?"

The sausage-seller isn't sophisticated. But he's a good man, a better man than Paphlagon, an honest man connected to real people because he is a real person himself. He cares about the public and knows the value and importance in government of "noble and good gentlemen." And he's bothered about social betterment, not just about himself. Before long, the demos recognize his worthiness, somehow comes to its wits, and is won over by the

sausage-seller's more earthy rhetoric, words of a mere-man rather
than those of a conceited, self-professed Godman like Paphlagon-
Cleon. Aristophanes would have needed to wait six centuries to
see his sausage-seller participate in Rousseau's *Social Contract*,
stalking its pages as "the public person," "formed by the union of
all other persons."

Rousseau's public person is an archetype of the social contract, a representative of the "reciprocal commitment" between an
individual and society. The public person singularly personifies
the demos much the same way as Aristophanes had it personified
in a single household. We can also read this person as a paradigm
of the reciprocal commitment we have seen break down in the
Anglosphere, gone because we know it's gone, because Rousseau
said its presence would make people "aware less of what belongs
to others than what does *not* belong to oneself." We're no longer
aware of this. And yet, reciprocal commitment is the bedrock of a
public value—the bedrock, moreover, of public virtue.

Rousseau never tells us how we might reach this virtuous
state, attain a society in which the social contract bonds together
its citizens, how it maintains the delicate balance between freedom and necessity. Nonetheless, he does give us a few hints about
what needs to be in place beforehand, and I'd caught glimmers
of this, in its modern everydayness, out on Seoul's streets: "Just
as the architect, before erecting a great building," says Rousseau,
"observes and plumbs the ground to see if it can bear the weight,
so the wise founder of institutions does not begin by drafting
laws good in themselves, but first examines whether the people
for which he intends them is capable of supporting them."

Fast-forward several hundred years, and we can see
Rousseau's public person reincarnated in Jane Jacobs's "public
character," her wily earth-spirit patrolling the sidewalks of *Death
and Life of Great American Cities* (1961). "The social structure

of the sidewalk," Jacobs says, "partly hangs on public characters," those men and women who have "frequent contact with
a wide circle of people." Storekeepers and barkeeps are obvious
public characters in city life (Joe Cornacchia, a deli owner along
her Hudson Street block, actually sells salamis!); yet there are
plenty of public characters anchored to the sidewalk, too, she
says, "well-recognized roving public characters."

Public characters know stuff and see things. They engage
in city affairs, even if it means sometimes sticking their noses
into these affairs, like Aristophanes's sausage-seller. Their main
qualification is that they *are* public, that they are visibly out in
public, in public spaces, there talking to lots of different people.
With public characters, "news travels that is of sidewalk interest."
Their presence helps create a certain "togetherness" in neighborhood life, connecting people to other people, spreading the word
"wholesale," Jacobs says, enlarging our notion of the public.

Rebuilding public institutions in the city will doubtless
require not a few public characters, helping reset both the public
and political mindset. Maybe, post-COVID, as an increasingly
outdoor, open-air urbanism takes hold, we can hope for a few
more sausage-sellers on the block, confronting the structures of
political power and demagogy, doing so in the new and necessary
agoras we've yet to invent. These al fresco street markets might
go back to the future and reenact our own version of Athenian
public-political theater whose dialogues and conversations, like
Aristophanes's, might prompt greater civic and critical awareness on the part of citizens and leaders. They'll both have their
legs pulled by the actors. Turning on us, the amused audience,
these actors might ask: *What are you laughing at? You're laughing at yourselves, that's what!*

Ah, if only life were that funny . . .

4

RADICAL URBAN HISTORY WITNESSED two noteworthy
anniversaries during the 2020–2021 lockdowns. Both never
really got their just celebratory deserts. The first was the fiftieth
birthday of Henri Lefebvre's best book on the city, *The Urban
Revolution* (1970); the second was our greatest ever urban revolution, the Paris Commune (1871), which toasted its one hundred and fiftieth when our cities were enduring a peacetime
bombardment. I want to talk more about each, quietly fête them,
because neither book nor event has lost any salience for helping
progressive people think about city life, even as COVID threatens that life. I might say *especially* as COVID threatens city life,
because *The Urban Revolution* and the Paris Commune offer
vital instruction about how we might rebuild a post-pandemic
urban world democratically.

The denigration of the city would have hardly surprised
Lefebvre. He knew about anti-urbanism and thwarted hopes.
*The Urban Revolution* was born of them, rooted and incubated
in the promise of 1968, yet anticipating much more the depressing era that would follow. By 1970, Lefebvre recognized that
the promise of those street-fighting years was dashed. A sober
reconceptualization was warranted, a taking stock, particularly
of material circumstances. What he foresaw, post-1968, was a
revolution fellow Marxist Antonio Gramsci might have labeled
"passive"—a revolt from above, a counter-revolution. (It's what
Marx meant in the *Manifesto* when he said, "the bourgeoisie has
played the most revolutionary part.") Still, what Lefebvre wanted
in *The Urban Revolution* was a revolution more akin to the Paris
Commune, something Gramsci would have called a "war of position," a popular, historical assault from below.

Lefebvre stands mainstream economic and sociological wisdom on its head: "We must consider industrialization as a stage of urbanization," he says. "In the double process (industrialization-urbanization), after a certain period, the latter term becomes dominant, taking over from the former." This is a bold, provocative statement for any Marxist, for it suggests that the mainstay of the capitalist economy isn't so much industrialization as urbanization, that industrialization all along was but a special form of urbanization. Capitalism reigns, Lefebvre says, because it manages and manufactures a very special commodity: *urban space*—an abundant source of surplus value as well as a massive means of production, a launch pad and rocket in a stratospheric global market.

We must speak of *urban society*, Lefebvre says, a society that shattered the internal intimacy of the traditional city, that grew into Frederick Engels' industrial city, but which has, in turn, been absorbed and obliterated by vaster metropolitan units. Rural places, too, become an integral part of the urban process, swallowed up by an "urban fabric" that continually extends its borders, ceaselessly corrodes the residue of agrarian life, gobbling up everything and everywhere to increase surplus value and accumulate capital. "This term, 'urban fabric,'" explains Lefebvre, "doesn't narrowly define the built environment of cities, but all manifestations of the dominance of the city over the countryside. In this sense, a vacation home, a highway and a rural supermarket are all part of the urban tissue."

*The Urban Revolution* appeared a year before Richard Nixon devalued the U.S. dollar, wrenching it from its gold standard mooring. Gone, almost overnight, was the financial and economic regulation that kept in check a quarter of a century of capitalist expansion. As the U.S. economy bore the brunt of war in Vietnam, an American balance of trade deficit loomed. Nixon knew fixed exchange rates couldn't be sustained without overvaluing the dollar and losing competitive ground. So he let the dollar drift, devalued it, and loosened Bretton Woods's grip. World currency oscillated after that; capital could now more easily slosh back and forth across national frontiers. A deregulated capitalism became rampant, without restraint; Lefebvre sensed its coming, and saw how it facilitated what he'd call the "secondary circuit of capital," a siphoning off of loose money that could more easily speculate on real estate and financial assets, liquid loot yearning to become concrete in space.

From capital's point of view, as a class, this makes perfect bottom-line sense: the landscape gets flagged out as a pure exchange value, and activities on land conform to the "highest," if not necessarily "best," land-uses. Profitable locations get pillaged as secondary circuit flows become torrential, just as other sectors and places are asphyxiated through disinvestment. Willy-nilly, people are forced to follow the money, to flow from the countryside into the city, from factories into services, from stability into fragility. The urban fabric wavers between devaluation and revaluation, crisis and speculative binge, a ravaged built form and a renewed built form—and a fresh basis for capital accumulation. Once, it was a gritty warehouse on a rusty wharf; now, it's a glitzy loft on a prim promenade. Once, an empty field on the edge; now, a core neighborhood on the up.

Half a century later, Lefebvre's insights in *The Urban Revolution* sound as fresh and meaningful as ever. Yet anybody expecting a rebel-rousing manifesto here will be disappointed. This isn't a book like *The Right to the City* (1968), which climaxed with a passionate "cry and demand" for urban life. In 1970, Lefebvre gave us a more reflective text, cautious in its militant musings. If we want clues about what kind of radical revolution *The Urban Revolution* does espouse, we must look backward, turn toward the past, and to an earlier Lefebvre work: *La proclamation de la Commune*, written in 1965. Reading it can help us move forward.

It was the *style* of the Commune that kindled Lefebvre's political imagination. What style? "The style of an immense, grandiose festival," he says, "a festival that citizens of Paris, essence and symbol of the French people and of people in general, offered to themselves and to the world. Festival at springtime, festival of the disinherited, revolutionary festival and festival of revolution, free festival, the grandest of modern times, unfurling for the first time in all its dramatic magnificent joy." For seventy-three days, loosely affiliated citizen organizations, neighborhood and artist associations, propped up by a "Central Committee" of the National Guard, transformed Paris's twenty *arrondissements* into a liberated zone of people power, freed from bourgeois authority, from its army and police, from its economy and bureaucracy.

In the early hours of March 18, 1871, a crowd of disgruntled citizens, predominately women, gathered on the Butte Montmartre and surrounded obsolete cannons that were public property. General Lecomte ordered the National Guard to seize the cannons, and to open fire. Three times he gave the order to shoot. The soldiers stood silent, reluctant to turn their weapons on their own, on "the people"; they *were*, after all, themselves "the people," conscripts from the working class, and before them stood their would-be mothers. It was a tense standoff. But suddenly, the tide turned. Machine guns would switch direction. They'd soon take aim at the rule of Order. Lecomte would be shot later that day, alongside General Clément Thomas, one of the chief executioners in the 1848 "June Days." Ten days on— March 28, 1871—in the Place de l'Hôtel-de-Ville, *la Commune de Paris* was formally proclaimed. "Here is the holy city," wrote Rimbaud not long afterward, "seated in the west."

It was, Lefebvre says, "grandeur and folly, heroic courage and irresponsibility, delirium and reason, exaltation and illusion" all rolled into one. Insurgents corroborated Marx's ideal of revolutionary praxis at the same time as they refuted it. For this was no worker uprising incubated in the factories; rather, "the grand and supreme attempt of a city raising itself to the measure of a human reality." An urban revolution had made its glorious debut, reenergizing public spaces and transforming everyday life, touting victory while it wobbled in defeat. It was condemned to death at birth, notwithstanding the gaiety of its baptism. "The movement's success," says Lefebvre, "masked its failings; conversely, its failures are also victories, openings onto the future, a standard to be seized, a truth to be maintained. What was impossible for the Communards stays until this day impossible, and, by consequence, behooves us to realize its possibility."

Ironically, the singularity and uniqueness of the Commune—that it occurred when Paris was besieged by war, surrounded by Prussian forces—makes it somehow more universally applicable for us today, as we, too, are besieged by forces that likewise surround us, that likewise invade our lives. In fact, the Commune's pre-history sounds ominously like our own present history. Poorer populations suffered the most. Paris's economy was kaput. Enterprises folded daily. Food was scarce. Unemployment grew. People stood in long lines outside essential services, like *boulangeries*, desperate for bread. Winter had been bleak. Spring stayed chilly. There was little fuel for heating. Meantime, the rich had fled, cleared off to the countryside, along with their money. The Bourse and the Banque de France equally upped sticks (and stocks); an interim bourgeois government ruled from Versailles.

This "de-structuring" of social life, says Lefebvre, rippled from top to bottom. On the other hand, its "re-structuring"—the reconstitution of urban life—flowed the other way, from the bottom upward. People reorganized and rebuilt Paris in the rubble, from the rubble. Here we can learn plenty. There was a moratorium on rents; debts were written off; parasitic practices forbidden. Paris was "*de*-capitalized." "There was a sort of qualitative bond," writes Lefebvre, "in the activity of the Parisian masses." The city's base became "the people of Paris ... artisans, small business owners, workers, petty-bourgeois allied to proletarians—who became spokespeople and participants in municipal events." These unsung heroes and heroines "were proud of their anonymity."

The promise of the city reveals itself here when all is taken away, when city life is most in danger. For what remains are only its human resources—its *citizens*, citizens acting as citizens, joining hands, participating, creating their own public institutions, organizing one another, doing so voluntarily, without monetary tags, without competitive compulsions; doing so, we might say, for the well-being of everybody else. It was the great gift of *cooperation* that Marx outlined in *Das Kapital*, his core vision of democracy. Marx spoke about cooperation at the workplace; here, we're talking about cooperating in an entire city, human beings pooling their will and wits as a municipal power. When people work together, Marx says, they "have hands and eyes both in front and behind, and can be said to be to a certain extent omnipresent." This is a rather lovely way to describe things. Marx thinks that when we "cooperate in a planned way with others," we strip off the fetters of our individuality "and develop the capabilities of our species."

But the problem with cooperation in "normal" capitalist life is its phoniness, that it's controlled exclusively by the bourgeoisie, by the ruling class, who exploit people's togetherness for their own commercial ends. Human omnipresence gets transformed into capital's omnipotence, a collective power, in other words, not mobilized for the common good but creamed-off as private gain. Marx calls it a "free gift" for business, an associative force that costs capital nothing. And "as cooperation extends its scale," he says, "the despotism of capital extends." That's the bad news. The good news is that "as the numbers of cooperating workers increases, so too does their resistance to the domination of capital." Marx always willed this at the factory; for seventy-three days, in Paris, in 1871, we glimpsed it in the street, in daily life, where we still need it most.

Could we ever imagine those extraordinary circumstances of Paris's Commune becoming somehow ordinary, actually embedded in a city life released from a competitive free-for-all? COVID instigated its own revolution in daily life, a passive, if deadly, revolution. But what of Lefebvre's active revolution, his right to the city? Could a de-commodified, de-capitalized city life ever become something completely normal? What if real cooperation became the order of day, that our hands and eyes were in the front and behind—as Marx suggested—and that we became "to a certain extent omnipresent"? We've seen what a strong state can do when it has to intervene in our economy and society, what it can do at a crisis moment, like under COVID, when it shut down businesses whether they liked it or not. Now we need to reimagine it intervening once the crisis has passed, intervening democratically, fostering cooperation and participation, enabling some bottom-up reconstruction of a world that has undergone so much top-down destruction. Perhaps afterward we might even see this state wither away.

One thing is clear: the right to the city no longer means the right of the rich and powerful to mobilize their property rights, to use them to abuse other people, to rip off at work and at home, to pay too little while charging too much. There must be some institutional control of flows into the secondary circuit of capital, some way those flows can be stymied, channeled into infrastructure and property geared toward public use-values, not corporate exchange-values. In Lefebvre's Marxist terminology, concrete space must prevail over abstract space. Those "blind-fields" of thinking of the world in terms of quantitative growth for quantitative growth's sake must be broken down, rendered longer-sighted, more socially visionary.

Lefebvre said the right to the city, if ever it came to pass, would resemble a giant social and spatial contract. Associative ties would bond people together, bond them to each other and to their city. In an age of public health crisis, we might add that these "rights" now need to be complemented by "duties." The Commune, again, is suggestive. Communards *gave* to the city, recognizing that they had responsibilities to make their city function. Public space wasn't just about *them*, exclusively about individuals. When they took their right to the city, they understood that public services meant public service, pivoted on respecting the collective, respecting each other in the realm of one another. Freedom here came through collective necessity, through contributing toward the common good—existentially profiting from this common wealth, primarily because people were helping create it themselves. The sense of unselfish achievement was legion. The value of the public realm was affirmed, kept robust and healthy.

The remarkable success story of the United Kingdom's vaccine roll out hinges on an unofficial subplot: the army of dedicated volunteers who chipped in to lend a cooperative hand, who organized the vaccination centers, the lineups and traffic flows; even the injections were often administered by voluntary nurses, doctors, and dentists going beyond the call of normal duty. And it was done everywhere with good cheer and with great efficiency. Maybe it's because collective participation offers personal fulfillment. Everybody knows it, everybody appreciates it and gets inspired by the positive spirit that was so evidently in the air. Waiting for your jab, standing in line, those hands and eyes in front and behind are really palpable and uplifting. One might dream of a public health system commandeering this much respect and person power in ordinary times.

Perhaps this collective feeling corresponds in a more modest way with what the Communards felt. It's a sensibility that crops up often in Lefebvre's *La proclamation de la commune* and is expressed by a word seldom spoken anymore: "dignity"—*la dignité*. We seldom hear it because so much of our life today, notably our urban life, has no dignity. It is *hard*, an alienating daily struggle to survive, to make ends meet. In among it all, dignity becomes a luxury, a far-off ideal, only something for the idle rich. But the sense of dignity, as the Communards knew, derives from solidarity, from public engagement. Poor but proud, they retained their dignity. They did the right thing, did it with others, staved off isolation and disempowerment and struggled to overcome adversity together. They sensed for a while that it could work, that you could succeed. Perhaps the right to dignity is really what *The Urban Revolution* quietly proclaims fifty years on, like the Commune, at its one hundred and fiftieth anniversary: *the right to be respected, the duty to respect others*. If there's ever a style worth emulating, then it's dignity. A grand style, for sure, that should never have gone out of fashion.

5

THERE'S SOMETHING ABOUT URBAN crowds, hordes of people in the city, in public. There's nothing like it, never will be. I miss being among people, lots of them. After months of lockdowns and isolations, I know I'm not the only one, that a lot of other people miss other people, too—not necessarily crowds of gaping tourists or zombies commuting *en masse* to work, but diversity and colors, shapes and faces, movement and dynamism, stuff that kindles our imagination, that challenges us, that makes modern city life tick, worth living; many friends have told me likewise, and many people have told my friends likewise as well.

Far from the madding crowd? I'm not so sure. That might've once been an ideal in people's heads and still is for some; and, of course, not a few people have sought this ideal out, fled cities for what they perceive as the relative safety and harmony of smaller towns and countryside, to say nothing about its affordability. Still, many others who've isolated themselves and become solitary citizens, are reassessing whether a life cut off is a deep-down human impulse.

Yet the concept of "far from the madding crowd" has persuasive sway over our collective psyche. We probably have the English novelist Thomas Hardy to thank for that—his *Far from the Madding Crowd*, published in 1874, an acclaimed masterpiece, Hardy's first literary success. There he played on Thomas Gray's poem "Elegy Written in a Country Churchyard," an eighteenth century lyric classic, much admired by T. S. Eliot, with its gentle meditation on the quietness of English rural life, on the forgotten dead in a graveyard: "Far from the madding crowd's ignoble strife," wrote Gray. "Their sober wishes never learn'd to stray; / Along the cool sequester'd vale of life / They kept the noiseless tenor of their way." But Hardy's book, a sunny one for him, atypical in its happy ending—Bathsheba succumbs to loving Gabriel and eventually marries him—is nonetheless unsettling, not quite what the title suggests.

Was Hardy ironizing? Likely, insofar as his is a text full of erotic energy and macabre scenes (like the corpses of a mother and baby), lulling unsuspecting readers out of any pastoral complacency and Victorian prudery. In fact, far from the madding crowd has plenty of "ignoble strife," and "the cool sequestered vale of life" is but a proxy for repressed violence and despair. With its fire and thunderstorms, life-threatening elemental eruptions and shooting, *Far from the Madding Crowd* might even be a staple read for our COVID age, bringing us closer to why madding crowds are so vital to being alive in the first place.

It was far from the madding crowd where I began to yearn for ignoble strife more than ever, for more noisy tenor to the quiet, secluded life I'd hitherto been compelled to lead. (I say "compelled" while recognizing the privilege of being able to withdraw.) In early summer 2021, after the first lockdown eased, I got into my car and drove to Hay-on-Wye, a famed "book town" in Powys, South Wales, right on the English border. The village is packed with used bookstores; they're literally everywhere, and in pre-COVID times Hay-on-Wye was renowned for its jammed literary festivals and vibrant bookfairs. The couple of days I spent worming its stores and thumbing its books, everything was eerily quiet, as if the end of the world were nigh, soon about to happen. And I often found myself alone in the stacks, communing quietly with characters in the text, much as I'd been doing for months at home.

The town's oldest book haven, founded in 1965, is the Hay Cinema Bookshop, a disused movie theater now a vast two-floor emporium of used, remainder, and antiquarian books, of all genres. If the two hundred thousand-odd volumes inside don't grab you, then outside, in a couple of gray steel containers, its bargain section will, with an array of sell-off and damaged books, many gems going for a song. Among them, I discovered a text that had a strange effect on me, not because of its writing but for what was on its cover. At first, I was appalled that someone would cast off such a handsome copy of F. Scott Fitzgerald's *A Life in Letters*, a big-formatted Penguin book published in 1998. Within its leaves is some marvelous correspondence between the author of *The Great Gatsby* and his daughter Scottie, then a student at Vassar College. "Some time when you feel very brave and defiant," Scott wrote Scottie, "and haven't been invited to one particular college function read the terrible chapter in *Das Kapital* on 'The Working Day,' and see if you are ever quite the same."

But these golden nuggets about Fitzgerald's radical politics didn't grip me quite like the beautiful glowing azur of Raoul Dufy's cover, a sweeping impressionistic vista of Nice, France, painted in 1926 from on high, from Castle Hill, with the city's famous Promenade des Anglais curving around the Mediterranean's Baie des Anges (Bay of Angels), disappearing into the distance at Cannes. There were palm trees and people, carriages and boats, sea and a yellowed-domed Casino (before it and its pier burned down)—an allure and romance that Dufy makes throb with his delicate brush. Some involuntary memory had suddenly been activated in my brain. I wanted to go there, desperately, to Nice, to enter this shifting scene, feel its energy, absorb people by the sea, remembering how, long ago, in the early 1980s, on a backpacking vacation, I'd once strolled down the Promenade des Anglais. Now, I needed to return, *had* to return.

Miraculously, two months later, in August, in the height of summer, pumped with vaccine, I was there again, back on a Promenade des Anglais flocked with people and boiling hot. I was walking along what must be one of Europe's greatest public spaces, stretching four miles from Quai des États-Unis (United States Quai) to Nice Airport, hugging a coastline and a sea the colors of which Dufy's paint hadn't exaggerated. All of us were mingling along the vast promenade that rich English Victorians had constructed in 1860. It was as if the sun were burning away

*Nice*

people's fears, cleansing the air of virus, lulling everybody, maybe, into a false sense of collective security.

In recent years, walkway space has increased, widened at the expense of traffic flows; dedicated bike lanes have also been put in place. Now, "La Prom" brings together every walk of life—buskers and ramblers, *flâneurs* and artists, roller-skaters and baby-strollers, wide-eyed tourists and seasoned locals, old and young alike—all walking and chatting, moving and sitting in a giant open-air democracy by the sea. It felt like uninterrupted liberty to move, to linger, to simply sit near a palm tree on one of the promenade's many fixed chairs and people watch, confirming William H. Whyte's homily about urban life: that the most fascinating thing for people in public is to observe other people in public.

To suck in its balmy, salty air, to imbibe the crowded vibe, was to photosynthesize amid an ocean of people. Strolling along, I felt like a character from Edgar Allan Poe, from his *Man of the*

*Crowd*—although I was pretty sure this sensibility wasn't exclusive to me or to men alone. We were all somehow "People of the Crowd." "For some months I had been ill in health," Poe had his protagonist tell us, "but was now convalescent." For some months, we'd all been ill in health, and now, here, the lucky ones were convalescing together, trying to recover from an illness that had shaken us to our existential core, that still might shake us to the core.

"Merely to breathe was enjoyment," Poe's hero says. "I felt a calm but inquisitive interest in everything." Again, I knew what he meant; I think a lot of others on the Promenade des Anglais knew what he meant, too. "Dense and continuous tides of population were rushing past . . . and the tumultuous sea of human heads filled me with a delicious novelty of emotion." Soon our man of the crowd contemplates, as I contemplated, "with minute interest the innumerable varieties of figure, dress, air, gait, visage, and expression of countenance." We were all "refusing to be alone," as Poe might have said. Maybe we were men and women yearning to be *close* to the madding crowd, dreaming of becoming *part* of it.

In Vieux Nice—the city's old town—throngs of people jostled one another, and energy levels were just as high as densities. In confined spaces, like lining up for ice cream at Gelateria Azzurro, along the narrow rue Sainte-Réparate, or grocery shopping at Cours Saleya's daily market, mask-wearing became more common. On these occasions, it's easy to understand why crowds and city streets have kindled the French literary imagination, becoming as much part and parcel of the French *vie quotidienne* as baguettes and red wine. In "Crowds," from *Le spleen de Paris* (1862), Baudelaire said, "a singular intoxication" awaits everyone who knows how "to take a bath in the multitude." Himself an avid admirer (and translator) of Edgar Allan Poe, Baudelaire likens this experience to a "universal communion," to a profane joy, the "feverish pleasure" of people discovering one another on a packed street. True enough. On the other hand, might we wonder whether Baudelaire's ideal of losing oneself in the crowd requires, under COVID, a more cautious reading: mightn't intoxication now be deadly, a feverish pleasure that poses grave dangers of losing yourself forever?

EPIDEMIOLOGISTS SAY COVID-19 "is primarily transmitted person-to-person by close contact through respiratory droplets." The scholarly journal *Communication Physics* (August 23, 2021) confirms, though, that "the role of population density is an open question with evidence for and against its influence on epidemic spreading." The journal says that "merely the density of contacts, while relevant at a neighborhood level, isn't enough to explain the mechanisms of spread." In a similar vein, the *International Journal of Environmental Research and Public Health* (September 2021), which features a detailed COVID study from Malaysia, reckons that (population density is a factor) in the spread of disease, yet caveats and riders remain. Density alone doesn't answer the fundamental question of why there's a "chaotic spread of disease at the population level."

Other studies highlight positive correlations between COVID and the "compactness of people." Yet, here again, there's no consensus on the direct effect of population density on the number of virus cases. The Malaysian survey showed that in districts with more than 250,000 inhabitants, and with a density of more than five hundred persons per square kilometer, approximately 1.5 people were infected with COVID—which is to say hardly any more than in less densely populated areas. Each time the population density increased by one individual per square kilometer, there was a tiny increase of 1.38 in the active COVID cases. The study said attack rates of the epidemic in some instances were higher in smaller districts than larger ones, a feature borne out in parts of China, suggesting there are "proxy drivers of contact rates."

The World Bank, too, released findings on the role of density and the spread of COVID, saying there's no direct causality between the two. "Density matters, but not much." The world's most densely populated cities in East and South-East Asia—for example, Seoul, Tokyo, Hong Kong, and Shanghai—have had low infection levels compared with sprawling U.S. cities. In China, cities with the highest infection rates were those with relatively low population densities, five thousand to ten thousand people per square kilometer.

In New York, the first wave of COVID killed more than

twenty thousand in a few months. Nobody knew what was happening. It seemed like a nightmare from the Middle Ages, black plague striking down everybody. How could people protect themselves? Run away? Pray for deliverance? People panicked, justifiably. Was it New York's openness, America's gateway to the world, with too many humans coming and going, that sparked mass infection? Was it the city's uniquely high population density, like Manhattan's whopping twenty-seven thousand people per square kilometer, together with its reliance on mass transit mixing? Or was it lifestyle, that New Yorkers always dined out and rarely stayed in? Maybe it was some combination of all these things? (Some of the city's highest infection rates were in lower-density Staten Island.)

As it transpired, Big Apple denizens soon wised up, began protecting themselves, started wearing masks, got vaccinated. Then came vaccine passes and more enlightened public health precautions. Ever since, the city has fared well on the health front, better than other places in America, better than many low-density cities like Dallas, even better than many small towns and rural areas. The city has gone on to suffer fewer COVID deaths than elsewhere in America, making it one of the nation's safer places for human life and limb.

All of which poses the question: are dense cities *per se* the problem when it comes to COVID? Maybe we should reframe this question: Is there any such thing as *per se* when we talk about cities? Aren't cities reflections of what is happening in our society, for better or worse? Don't our economics and politics get inscribed in city life, flourish in cities, get intensified in cities, often plague cities? To attribute causation to cities *in themselves*, in other words, is to fetishize the city, is to misinterpret how cities are both reflectors and shapers of wider social and cultural processes. Sometimes cities exacerbate social woes; elsewhere, they might be palliative or even curative for those woes. It all depends. To give up on cities, to run away from them, to wag the finger at them, strikes me as problematic. We need a different conversation about cities and our society and about our society in cities.

High-density crowds, of course, are one of the great virtues of cities, perhaps *the* greatest virtue, the innumerable encounters between different people and the sociability that prevails from this diversity. Sometimes sociability doesn't prevail; conflict rules—social breakdown and separation. Yet maybe the dilemma of COVID urbanism isn't so much about crowd avoidance as *crowd management*, about how one responds to the crowd, in the crowd, how people act toward one another, respect (or disrespect) one another (through mask-wearing, social distancing, etc.), how people understand themselves as people in public, not as individuals simply doing what you like among people. How do democratic institutions respond to crowds? How do they manage (or mismanage) crowds, safeguard a general will while protecting against the flouting of individual rights? How ought the police react to crowds, to peaceable and legitimate mass comings together? Something crucial in any crowd management is differentiating between crowds and *crowding*, especially *overcrowding*. What we're talking about here is overcrowding that scars everyday urban living for many people.

Overcrowding is different than density; the two terms shouldn't be used interchangeably; they're distinguishable. Overcrowding can be just as palpable in low-density areas as in high-density ones, and high-density doesn't necessarily equate to overcrowding. Plenty of the world's richest neighborhoods—like Manhattan's Upper East Side or Monte Carlo—are mega-dense yet *not* overcrowded. (Monte Carlo is second on the world's densest urban roster and perhaps the wealthiest, with a 32 percent multi-millionaire population!) Overcrowding is where households have more occupants than rooms (excluding bathrooms) and where people can't avoid close contact with each other. As many multi-occupants tend to be poorer, and their jobs more menial, they don't have the luxury of homeworking, either. And even if they did, they'd have nowhere at home to work. Occupants come and go at all hours, depending on work shifts, and expose themselves and their housemates to people at large, to greater risk of infection.

A study in Chicago found no correlation between population density and COVID infection rates (see "In Chicago, Urban Density May Not Be to Blame for Spread of the Coronavirus," *ProPublica*, April 30, 2020). But it did find a direct link between *overcrowding* and infection. "The communities hardest hit by the virus in Chicago," the report says, "are low-density black and Hispanic neighborhoods, including ones where economic decline and population loss have caused more people to live in the same household."

In Englewood, a Chicago neighborhood hit especially hard by the 2008 housing market collapse, foreclosures and dwindling affordable stock have left less-resourced denizens with few options. Home ownership is off-limits; ditto high-rental units. So many people, particularly younger people, are forced to live with relatives, parents or aunties and uncles who, decades ago, could muster the means to buy into the city's housing stock. "There's a lack of basic life essentials in the community," one local politician says. "This is the culmination of decades of disinvestment." "This is not about disparities in behavior or preventable cases of COVID, where, if people just knew more information, they'd be social distancing." "It's really a sad tale of people who know what's coming, but there's nothing they can do about it unless you give them housing or get them out of this predicament."

Even before COVID struck, the *Guardian* warned of

"Shoebox Britain," of "how shrinking homes are affecting our health and happiness" (October 10, 2018). Britain's speculatively induced housing crisis has pushed more and more people into homes that are shrinking and multi-occupied. The slicing and dicing up of houses and office buildings has been ongoing for a while, recalling the dark, Dickensian era of tenements and rookeries, only it's twenty-first-century style. The walls are closing in for many people, and there's no way out, especially during a pandemic. Home offers no escape, no refuge or haven in an anxious world. Only confinement, engineered by market-driven expansion, resulting in a sense of isolation and claustrophobia inside that's almost as hazardous to human health as the outside. It is overcrowding spawned by inequality, by greed, an introverted low-density overcrowding, economically manufactured, far removed from the extrovert delights of the high-density crowd.

"Shoebox Britain" slams decades of neoliberal urban policies. Successive government ministers (irrespective of political persuasion) have relaxed planning regulations and encouraged more and more housing development that's rarely "affordable." Developers and landlords always find loopholes in these regulatory changes for corner-cutting and boosting profits. Meanwhile, local authorities, desperate for alternatives to their dwindling housing stock, have little choice but to steer needy residents over to these exploitative private landlords. And given there are few resources to monitor the quality of accommodation, it's invariably squalid, a threat to physical as well as mental health.

Curiously, Britain's neoliberal cities had "lockdown" policies well before anybody heard of COVID. For years, rogue landlords and developers have been converting—locking-down—single-family homes into tiny apartments for housing benefit claimants. By including a token shared facility, like a minuscule kitchen, these developments are treated as internal apartment shares and

planning permission can be bypassed. The rental streams generated from six crappily constructed studios are exponentially
greater than a three-bedroomed share in the same property. And
it's the taxpayers who line the landlord's pockets because the
state is effectively picking up the rental tab. Is this "warehousing"
of human life likely to protect anybody under COVID? Is it ever
likely to enhance human well-being post-COVID? It's hard to
imagine, unless something changes, unless greater space, affordability, and dignity can be established in urban living. Cities need
to thrive on collective use values, not wither as privately appro-
priated exchange values.

6 studio apartment of 1  3 bedroom

SINCE TIME IMMEMORIAL, DEBATES have unfurled about the
relationship between density and crowding and the health of city
dwellers. More insightful past commentators, like social psychologist Jonathan Freedman, argue that density and crowding are
neither good nor bad. Instead, says Freedman, in his still-valuable
*Crowding and Behavior* (1975), crowding and density intensify
the effects of preexisting social situations, much as COVID has
intensified preexisting social situations. High-density crowding
does affect people, yet its effects depend on other factors in the
situation. High density, says Freedman, might cause people to be
friendlier but also less friendly, just as crowding might produce
great mutuality and greater malaise. Crowding can be negative
when it creates its dialectical other of isolation and stress, when
overcrowding is pressured and forcible; yet crowding might elsewhere mean the vitality of having many people about, constant
"eyes" on busy streets (as Jane Jacobs liked to emphasize), ensuring social interaction and neighborhood safety.

If a social situation is bad, says Freedman, when people feel
cut off and vulnerable, economically deprived, high density will

likely aggravate an already fraught situation. Poorer people often feel powerless, subject to forces beyond their control, and living in a badly maintained high-rise with hundreds of peers might exaggerate feelings of uninhabitability. In this context, density and crowding, rather than poverty and inequality, are conveniently blamed for any social pathology. Conversely, if the situation is structured so that people aren't cut-off or withdrawn, and a building or neighborhood nurtures positive feelings of empowerment and collaboration, cheerier outcomes might ensue. Better things might even get encouraged by high-density crowding.

This was always William H. Whyte's central point in his pioneering *The Last Landscape* (1968), a book that boldly makes "the case for crowding." (Since his bestseller from the late fifties, *The Organization Man*, "Holly" Whyte had consistently been a thorn in the side of conventionality; he was also a staunch early advocate of Jane Jacobs, helping kickstart her career.) Whyte says official U.S. land policy, as elsewhere, has invariably been contra higher density; "decentralist" by nature, with the primary thrust of "moving people outward; reducing densities, loosening the metropolis, and reconstituting its parts in new enclaves on the fringe."

But Whyte isn't advocating stacking everybody up in giant towers. High density, he says, doesn't mean *only* high-rise; a tight-knit patterning of low buildings can exhibit surprisingly high rates of people per acre, sometimes even greater than twenty-story towers placed apart, where interstitial spaces are frequently empty and institutional, hardly inviting for lingering or leisure. They're wastes of space, dead zones. Whyte wants to fill them with vitality, with healthy congestion.

Here he similarly draws the distinction between "overcrowding"—too many people per room—and density—the numbers of people per acre. "Overcrowding does make for an unhealthy environment," Whyte reckons, whereas "high density may or may not." Besides, he says, everyone is always bemoaning the bad consequences of overcrowding, but what, he wonders, about "undercrowding"? "Researchers would be a lot more objective if they paid as much attention to the possible effects on people of relative isolation and lack of propinquity. Maybe some of those rats they study get lonely too?"

The thesis is challenging in an age of COVID, when crowding has aided the proliferation of infection rates while at other times has offered an antidote, the potentiality of a mutual aid, bulwarking the spread of infection. Unsurprisingly, apart from the deadly effects of physical illness, COVID has traumatized people's psychological well-being, too. Medical practitioners now speak of a "second pandemic," the chronic anxieties and depressions afflicting populations, especially those witnessing high body counts. The phenomenon has stimulated a lot of research into how lockdowns have disrupted communities and heightened loneliness, their impact hardest on people already socially, economically, and medically vulnerable. The evidence is clear enough: social distancing has stressed mental health, yet it has unfolded differently in high-density neighborhoods compared to those where conditions of "undercrowding" and "overcrowding" persist.

What's happened in Britain is typical of what's happened everywhere: an upsurge in community and voluntary activism, a "social cure" to pandemic fallout, and having ordinary citizens collectively resolve their own problems. Up and down the United Kingdom, resident groups and community associations, alongside legions of volunteers, have forged "COVID-19 Mutual Aid Groups," stepping in to provide practical and emotional support in neighborhoods where government and private sector programs haven't reached. Sociability here has bolstered mental health, helped counteract so-called "corona-related loneliness."

Notably, communities that have coped best with COVID tend to be more cohesive and selfless; residents there have a stronger sense of belonging and attachment to place. And frequently, they're located in densely populated urban areas. High-density neighborhood propinquity seems to accord more opportunities for mutual aid. The experience of a collective fate has led to a collective bonding that tries to change this fate.

A British study called "The Mental Health Benefits of Community Helping During Crisis," published in *The Journal of Community and Applied Social Psychology* (April 5, 2021), discovered that for enhancing well-being, "unity is essential." Their findings suggest that, perhaps somewhat paradoxically, crowding doesn't so much spread infection as provide a social prophylactic to counteract it. Another study from Italy ("COVID-19 in Our Lives," *Journal of Community Psychology*, December 20, 2021) reiterated the point, adding how a "feeling of responsibility" to protect the community was also consistent with adherence to nationwide social distancing policies. A sense of belonging and a sense of responsibility enabled individuals and groups "to look at uncertainty, both dampening it and managing it." "If a person's tie with a community includes the feeling of responsibility for what happens," the study said, "individuals will feel the desire to act and reflect on what to do to maintain a connection with their community."

Research carried out in Spain on "The Role of Sense of Community in Harnessing the Wisdom of Crowds" (*Journal of Business Research*, November 12, 2021) echoed these takeaways. But here, the notion of "crowding" assumes another inflection. The crowds in question were virtual and constituted people who participated in "crowdsourcing" in the "co-creation" of knowledge. They were individuals communicating and collaborating with each other via online groups. The concept is that in times of COVID emergency, the "collective mind" can generate greater wisdom and mobilize itself more effectively. It was precisely this hypothesis that Spanish researchers wanted to test out, examining the efficacy of a sample of virtual communities who'd "achieved a high level of social interaction when face-to-face communication wasn't possible."

Social media, they say, drew together various "stakeholders" and "allowed crowds to launch online communities, sharing feelings and information and even contributing to the resolution of individuals' concerns and problems, eventually reducing feelings of loneliness and promoting positive values." It's not clear how these virtual communities might ever be converted into offline associations, doing practical work in kind, post-COVID, rather than just over the airwaves, on the computer screen. Does the immaterial ever materialize into real place-based crowdsourcing?

Moreover, it'd be interesting to know if crowdsourcing flourished in conditions of undercrowding, if it helped reduce physical isolation and disempowerment. Maybe crowdsourcing works best in neighborhoods where stronger senses of real community already prevail. Nevertheless, the mitigating effects of virtual communication are apparent—the human contact, the *conversation*, the emotional care and the empathetic solidarity were all real enough, sustaining people during confinement. Curiously, the researchers also confirmed how "the wisdom of the crowds was an effective solution for identifying misinformation and verify fake news and alternative facts."

The virtual crowd will never replace the crowd in the street, the physicality of bodies, bodies really co-present in space. It'll never replace it for me anyway. Crowds offer energy releases, glorious and often maddening comings together of individuals and groups—crowds of protesters and demonstrators, crowds of shoppers and aimless strollers. Sometimes crowds can be led astray, manipulated, deceived *en masse*, warped by advertising and misinformation, sheepishly following one another, rallied on by demagogy; other times, crowds dramatize the power people lack, express *real* truths about injustice and voice political ambitions before the political means necessary to realize them are created. Either way, the crowd on the street is different from the crowd on the screen. ("A fire in the street ain't like a fire in the hearth," says Frank Zappa.) There's a special texturing to masses of people in the open air, in the sunshine, even in the rain, an electricity generated by pure physical encounter.

That said, maybe the sensibility of the online group and the "weak ties" that ensue don't only *simulate*; perhaps they can also *stimulate* awareness of real crowds and the strong ties of emergent public citizens? Perhaps a willingness to join crowdsourcing reflects a greater readiness to want to join the crowd, a desire to participate socially and politically, to go beyond a private self hemmed in by two dimensions and four walls. The Spanish crowdsourcing researchers said their participants "felt connected with crowds, sensed that individuals belong to the community, and built close friendship ties among participants." "*Feeling loyal to the crowd*," they said, "contributed to finding common ground in cohesion and compatibility." (The emphasis is mine.) "It provided mutual support and promoted collaboration and teamwork to foster resilience in the face of a pandemic."

"Feeling loyal to the crowd" is an exciting term. Maybe it's another way of voicing Baudelaire's ideal of "peopling your solitude," of not only losing yourself in the crowd but finding yourself, feeling at home even when you're not at home, doing it safely, healthily. Baudelaire's register is romantic and melancholic, yet it's somehow more optimistic than Thomas Hardy's. Maybe it's more comforting, too, less threatened by the madding crowd, about the human merging that takes place in urban life, about the experience "of being oneself and someone else," as Baudelaire says, "adopting every profession, every joy, every misery, as one's own."

The psychic rewards are enormous. "What people call love is awfully small," writes Baudelaire near the end of "Crowds," "awfully restricted, and awfully weak, compared with that ineffable orgy, that holy prostitution that gives itself totally, poetry and charity, to the unexpected that appears, to the unknown that passes by." Merging with the urban crowd won't ever prevent a pandemic, nor will it fully resolve the sadness and loneliness at the core of much human life. But it might help us understand each better, help us absorb our sorrows and celebrate our joys. It might shed light on dark shadows and enlarge the horizon of our being alive.

6

WHEN WE THINK OF CROWDS in cities, we perhaps instinctively think of main drags in cities, of Main Streets and High Streets, of chief thoroughfares and grand boulevards, of Great White Ways and Promenades des Anglais, of spaces and places that everybody knows, that captivate people, that draw people together, that entice and light up the night. "It's always night," jazz musician Thelonious Monk used to say, "or we wouldn't need light." Main Streets bring such light to cities, to large and small cities everywhere. Main Streets light things up and bring luminescence to people's darkest lives. In the biggest, brightest cities, there might be many main streets alongside *the* Main Street.

One of our most informed scholars of Main Street is the American urbanist and social psychologist Mindy Thompson Fullilove. In 2020, Fullilove released a book she'd been working on for eleven years: *Main Street*, with its revealing subtitle: *How a City's Heart Connects Us All*. Scouring the Main Streets of 178 cities in fourteen countries, Fullilove's mission here was "to discern the contribution of Main Street to our collective mental health." Implicit in her book is a warning that after social distancing is lifted, business-as-usual economic distancing must never return. Those old inequities, the short-term greed and divisions that pervade our society, manufactured by our leaders, can no longer cut it.

*Main Street* was written before COVID, appearing just as lockdowns were turning off Main Streets' lights. The shutters were going down on all "non-essential businesses"; some of the smallest would never pull them up again. An early casualty was Fullilove's beloved Irish pub-restaurant, Coogan's, in upper Manhattan's Washington Heights, closing its doors under the March 2020 lockdown, never to reopen. (Coogan's former owner, Peter Walsh, has pledged to fight for small businesses throughout America and has already raised $100,000 in support funds.) Many Main Streets will require financial lifelines. Fullilove's book is important because it shows why Main Streets lived on so vibrantly in the first place and why it is vital for our public health to keep them alive and resuscitate those terminally sick.

When *Main Street* hit the bookstands, I was asked to participate in its launch, to say a few words at a Zoom virtual event, this time involving a hundred-plus fellow travelers tuning in across global time zones, drifting in from Japan and France, from the United Kingdom, onward over both U.S. coasts. Although the real epicenter of the encounter was Orange, New Jersey, Fullilove's hometown, base camp for her political and educational exploits. Friends, family, and the diverse array of people who have been touched and influenced by her work, including several New Jersey town mayors, all joined in the virtual proceedings, fêting

Fullilove. If ever there were awards for a New Jersey "organic intellectual" (in the Gramscian sense), Fullilove would bag the lot each year.

*Main Street* is another installment of Fullilove's attempt to ward off bad urban karma. She may hail from the East Coast yet acts like the Good Witch of the North, knowing that behind every evil spell lies a counter-spell to undo it, one that can change the course of the hurricane. She knows that while there are plenty of evil spells fracturing U.S. neighborhoods and public life, counter-spells can unite them; that while evil spells create division and hate, counter-spells spread joy and love; that while evil spells turn life into a dark puzzle, counter-spells unpuzzle, make life collectively human and thrilling.

I first encountered Fullilove years back, on the page, and it came with a *Wow!* factor. Actually, it wasn't so much within the text as on the cover—of her book *Root Shock* (2004): a blurb from the legendary urbanist Jane Jacobs. I mean, a blurb from Jane Jacobs! *Wow!* Jacobs had only a year or so left to live, but one of the greatest urban scholars had this to say of another: "By practicing good science in a fallow field, Fullilove illuminates her chosen subject and also transcends it." Jacobs knew a good egg when she saw one.

Fullilove does practice good science because, unlike most other urbanists, where PhDs are a dime a dozen, she's a *real* doctor, a trained medical doctor, a fully qualified psychiatrist. Yet a peculiar breed of doctor at that. Indeed, rather than cash in on all those expensive years of medical school, setting up some cushy private practice in a rich part of town (the fallow field Jacobs talks about), Fullilove has done something more novel and noble instead: toiled for public betterment in a poor part of town.

In the early 1990s, in a cramped Washington Heights office,

she belonged to a small yet dynamic multidisciplinary team called the Community Research Group (CRG), part of Columbia University's School of Public Health and the New York State Psychiatric Institute. Their laboratory was right outside the doorstep, on gritty upper Manhattan streets. All around her then swirled every imaginable urban epidemic (some, we know now, weren't yet imaginable), from AIDS and crack addiction to mental illness-related violence and multi-drug-resistant tuberculosis. Walking to work, Fullilove remembered, meant negotiating sidewalks littered with crack vials. Unsettling as the experience was, it was somehow inspirational, too.

In those years, New York was still grappling with fiscal crisis and deindustrialization, with decline and hard drugs, just as banks and Wall Street piled up speculator profits. Yet Fullilove and her co-workers were dealing with an urban rot rooted in the fifties, with its large-scale urban renewal programs. James Baldwin had called this urban renewal "Negro Removal," since of the one million displaced, 63 percent were African American. Other policy nostrums during the sixties and seventies further threatened life and limb of low-income urban dwellers, both black and white. One was "benign neglect," the not-so-bright idea of Richard Nixon's urban affairs advisor Daniel Patrick Moynihan. Nothing "benign" here. This was the *purposeful* running down of disadvantaged neighborhoods, those too much of a public burden to fix. "Malign neglect," critics termed it, emphasizing the active pathology of the process. Its partner in urbicidal crime was "planned shrinkage," Roger Starr's brainchild, "planning" the elimination of "bad"—read: poor, minority—neighborhoods across America.

The paradigmatic case study of planned shrinkage was New York's South Bronx. Fire trucks were too costly to keep putting out all those fires. So let's shut down the stations! Fullilove's colleague and mentor-epidemiologist at CRG, Rodrick Wallace, argued that planned shrinkage in the South Bronx unleashed a "synergism of plagues." It wasn't one plague in particular but a whole accumulation of them, each conspiring together to have a catastrophic effect on inner-city neighborhoods; a complex mix of how bad urban policy creates bad environments and how bad environments became toxic for people with few resources to cope. Service cuts prompted severe housing deterioration, landlord arson, and even worse overcrowding—a breeding ground for AIDS, tuberculosis, and other infectious diseases. The cycle became vicious; urban decay had become contagious, a public health nightmare.

Starr himself poisoned the air every time he put ink on the page and opened his mouth, either as urban affairs commentator at *The New York Times* or as New York's Housing Commissioner. (Jane Jacobs called Starr "a fool.") He launched tirades against "community," insisting that the principle doesn't exist in urban America. Since there's no such thing, blocks could be blasted (enter Robert Moses), and people moved on a whim. "American neighborhoods can be disassembled and reconstituted as readily as freight trains," Starr wrote. "Stretches of empty blocks may be knocked down, services can be stopped and the land left fallow until a change in economic and demographic assumptions makes the land useful again." He cited a report on Boston called *Grieving for a Lost Home*, which "found that 26 percent of women relocated were emotionally disturbed two years after the move." "Were they not 'emotionally disturbed' before moving?" Starr wondered. Those who attack urban renewal, he said, "have inferred that people living in areas to be renewed—where rents are low and physical deficiencies high—actually are well satisfied with their homes. With this assumption, I find myself in rather serious disagreement."

Fullilove, of course, was in serious disagreement with Starr's serious disagreement. In her scientific work, she'd spent much time talking to people who'd lost their homes through various urban policies. "What they had described to me," she says, "was a wrenching feeling of disconnection, accompanied by disorientation at first, followed by alienation and nostalgia." Yet this was nostalgia "in the psychiatric sense," she stresses, "a profound and even life-threatening grief caused by the loss of home. I labeled this *root shock*." She'd borrowed the language from gardeners. They use the term to describe how carelessly moving plants from one site to another, severing roots, is deadly. Plants can't tolerate transplantation, and neither can people. "It was a regular part of people's stories," Fullilove says, "that old people died when the neighborhood was uprooted. They couldn't take the move."

I remember reading *Root Shock* and recalling my own brush with people getting uprooted. It came when I was five years old. Needless to say, I didn't know it then, hadn't experienced it directly; but Fullilove would later help me piece it together. It was 1965 when my grandmother and grandfather were shipped off to Cantril Farm, a brave new housing project on the fringes of Liverpool, in the United Kingdom. There were several problems with this shipping off. For one thing, my grandmother, grandfather, and their daughter, my aunt Emily, my mother's younger sister, were all shipped off *whether they liked it or not*; they weren't given a choice in the matter, just a letter in the mail. The letter told them their house was condemned, deemed a slum, and they would have to move out soon. Their little inner-city row house on Holden Street in Toxteth—their prim and proper, if poor, little row house on a block rich in social relations and mutual support systems—was deemed squalid by urban "experts."

Yet even before it was finished, Cantril Farm was falling apart. Tower blocks were leaky and damp; there was little sound insulation between apartments; communal corridors smelled of urine, lacked lighting, and what lighting there was often didn't work; elevators were frequently broken. There was no public transport, no doctors' surgeries, no stores, no Main Street, no nothing—a high-rise wilderness set in a wilderness, a fallow field in a fallow field, cut off from anywhere, from any memorable past and any discernible future. It was row upon row of austere breeze-block towers, homes for twenty thousand wounded denizens, mushrooming on land the council acquired at a snip. Little wonder my grandmother didn't last long in this wilderness, nor my grandfather. Both died a few years later of broken hearts within a broken community. Soon after, my thirty-something Aunt Emily developed ovarian cancer. She was dead by forty. As a five-year-old, I knew nothing; later, I heard words describing this life- and death-form: *alienation, alienated life*, initiated by nameless, faceless professionals. Now, though, I know it was *root shock*.

Such root shock was probably one subliminal reason why I took up an interest in urban affairs and why *Root Shock* left a lasting impression on me. It was another decade before I first encountered Fullilove herself, in person, at New York's New School, where she'd just begun teaching. I'd been invited there by the architect Bill Morrish, Fullilove's new colleague, who cameos in *Main Street*. Morrish asked me to talk about the plight of capitalist cities, and I'd probably said more than he'd asked for, maybe even spoken too downbeat. I wasn't seeing much intrigue or novelty in urban life anymore, nor much democracy. Our cities are increasingly unfair and uninteresting, flattened by familiarity, even as those glitzy skyscrapers go up, especially as they go up.

Past decades have seen colossal urban expansion. At the same time, the parameters for human expansion, for the expansion of the self, have diminished, dwindled for many denizens. Cities gorge on capital and wealth. The rich plunder urban land as a lucrative financial asset, expelling a residue of people priced out, displacing and uprooting them. It's something of a global phenomenon, happening everywhere. I said that maybe we could see this growing residue as a sort of *shadow citizenry* of disenfranchised people, who carry within their *shadow passports*, unofficial documentation expressive of a phantom solidarity, a solidarity people themselves hadn't yet recognized.

I wasn't sure what the audience would make of such a flight of fancy. I'd brandished the idea partly in jest, as a provocation, and partly as a metaphor to get people imagining. But afterward, somebody approached who'd been listening intently, knowingly. Introducing herself, it was Mindy Thompson Fullilove, and all of a sudden, from her own secret sleeve, she thrust before me a real-life shadow passport! Another *Wow!* The thing resembled a genuine U.S. passport—same size, same thickness, same bald eagle seal. And yet, it was bright orange colored, and inside its back flap, swashbucklingly dressed, was a Puss-in-Boots mascot, with the accompanying caption: "Sound Mind in a Sound Body in a Sound City." Here, then, was my first glimpse of the illicit travel papers of the University of Orange, in Orange, New Jersey.

Situated in an African American community, since 2008, the university has been open to all comers, to people for whom "official" paying universities are firmly shut, beyond budget. Its faculty, including Fullilove herself, is wholly volunteer; the classroom isn't so much about teaching as sharing experience, a dynamic dialogue between student and instructor, discussing civic engagement and community participation. Students earn "Be Free" degrees by taking classes, voting in elections, attending town meetings, and volunteering to do something in the community, even if it's just sweeping trash off the sidewalk. With each community duty fulfilled, the holder's passport is stamped; each stamp counts as a credit toward graduation. With this shadow passport, bearers learn how to scamper through the brambles of life.

The University of Orange figures prominently in Fullilove's book *Urban Alchemy* (2013). One of her best spells in this magical bag of tricks is no hocus pocus. It insists that communities discover what they're *for*, find something that might bring people together in a positive sense, affirm the creative, not merely denounce the negative. Part of this magic is earthily unmagical: it asks communities to look within themselves, to see what they've already got, to reclaim their *hidden assets*, not just commiserate over their more obvious deficits. It's as simple and complex as ABCD—Asset-Based Community Development. Find solidarity, celebrate your achievements, no matter how small or seemingly insignificant.

*Urban Alchemy* witnessed Fullilove becoming more poetic and impressionistic, more personal and, as such, maybe even more political than before. She edges her science toward social science, her philosophy toward spiritualism, all the while waving her characteristic Good Witch wand of generosity and compassion. Such is the timely spirit that infuses *Main Street*, too, a companion volume to her two previous works, the fulfillment of an urban trilogy, pursuing once again the theme of what's wrong and what's right about urban America. I say this thinking of Scott Fitzgerald's passage from *The Crack-Up*, that "the test of a first-rate intelligence is the ability to hold two opposed ideas in mind at the same time, and still retain the ability to function. One should, for example, be able to see that things are hopeless and yet be determined to make them otherwise."

Never has modern society been so full of conjuring tricks as today, carried out by self-serving politicians. They've cast spells the likes of which we've never seen before. They've become sorcerers of collusions and conspiracies, tricks and deceptions, fear and loathing, fake news and endless, unbelievable sleights of the economic and political hand that have become, alas, all too believable. *Main Street* thus appears as an anti-hate manifesto, the kind of counter-magic we need to help transform us back into thinking and caring human beings. Within its pages, we hear a diverse array of gentle voices and honest testimonies—from friends and family, mentors and colleagues, poets and philosophers, clergymen and cardiac patients. "When we go to Main Street," Fullilove writes, "we take in fashion, culture, and sociability. We shop, mail letters, get library books, and have coffee . . . Sometimes we take our laptops to be in the flow and in the know while ostensibly working. This makes us happy. It is a Machine for Living."

Main Streets are like canaries in a coal mine. If the canary lives, you can bet the mine has a rich abundance of nuggets; if the bird suffocates, you know the air is dead. When Main Streets disappear, the center disappears, Fullilove says, and people are propelled into a "centrifugal crisis." Main Streets are intricately ordered microcosms of a bigger macrocosm; their mutual survival depends on their coexistence. "When parts of a region have collapsed," Fullilove argues, "this has consequences for the region as a whole. . . . We ignore the reality that the prosperous parts also suffer when segments of the city are allowed to fester. There are useful parallels to what happens to people in the aftermath of a stroke, when they might ignore the affected part, acting as if it were not there."

Main Streets form capillaries of a living, breathing, palpitating organism. Fullilove's Main Streets are full of cells and soft tissue, where streets are arteries that need to flow to nourish the entire body politic. But Main Streets also need independent structuring, a particular set of architectonics to function healthily. They'll require clear demarcations, specific relationships to surrounding buildings, and definite lines and borders. And yet, Main Streets need open and porous borders that loop and curl into backstreets, that have walkable links to adjacent communities, accessible transit connections all around. Main Streets need to be discrete yet shouldn't be *too* discrete: they can't be ghettos hacked off from the rest of the city, engulfed on all sides by busy highways.

Fullilove has drifted through a lot of Main Streets, walked them, observed, talked to people, ordinary people as well as professional practitioners. Although she got to pace many miles of New York's Broadway and ate French patisseries as a *flâneuse* in Gay Paree, sipped çay in Istanbul and chilled in Kyoto's dazzling Zen temples, her real concern is Main Street, USA, the more modest main stems of provincial America. There, she paints her canvas as sensitively as Edward Hopper, yet touching up with a few hues he'd left out. There, she has us journey to, among other places, Baltimore and Brattleboro, Charlottesville and Cleveland, Memphis and Minneapolis, Salt Lake City and St. Louis. Many more of her Main Streets are closer to home, in New Jersey—in Asbury Park (with its famed boardwalk, serenaded by Bruce Springsteen) and Englewood, in Jersey City and Livingston, in Maplewood and Newark, in Tenafly, and, of course, in Orange.

If Main Streets are magnets for people, they need something that attracts. We know the cumulative effects of people attracting other people. But what stimulates people to come in the first place? When Main Streets work, says Fullilove, it seems obvious and natural why they work. But in reality, Main Streets are complicated public spaces. They can be desolate as well as vibrant, threatening as well as thriving. It's a delicate mix. But there are specific ingredients, a "tangle" of key characteristics (not one) that usually make Main Streets succeed, that have them tick around the clock. For a start, they'll have "standing patterns of behavior." "What we do on Main Street," she says, "will be consistent with what we think Main Street is."

People dress for Main Street; they moderate their noise to fit the scene; they expect to be entertained, somehow. They go shopping, do the daily rounds, but going there is more than simply shopping, more than going to the local mall, which isn't a public space, and doesn't tolerate the people and activities you see on Main Street: panhandlers and protests, general lounging and hanging out, kids running for the bus and little old ladies crossing the street. Main Street bears the same artistry that Claes Oldenburg harked about in 1961. They embroil themselves with everyday crap and still come out on top; they tell you the time of day; they unfold like a map that you can squeeze, like your sweety's arm, or that you can kiss, like a pet dog.

Some on Main Street hold themselves with dignity; others don't. It's a civic responsibility to determine what is acceptable behavior and what's not. The setting should be designed to fit and support the action, says Fullilove, and allow for behavior to happen; and its happening, in turn, supports more behavior. She says busy and hospitable Main Streets frequently have a "box" quality. They're clearly enclosed—though we're not talking about a roof here—with an attractive street "wall" and decent signage. There needs to be ample sidewalk capacity, too, with no impediments for pedestrians, like parking lots or cars turning, cutting into walker space. The box matters, Fullilove says, because it helps concentrate buildings and serves an efficiency. People can get things done within it. They recognize a coherence to their surrounding landscape and act upon it. Still, enclosure can't be too restricted to militate against permeability. It has to enable seamless comings and goings, chance encounters to take place. Main Streets require finely balanced combos of openings and enclosures.

That doesn't mean they can't be big or without traffic—New York's Broadway, after all, one of the world's most famous main

streets, stretching 13.4 miles, is also a busy automobile artery—
so long as there's an imageability and demarcation, lines that
define it, that let pedestrians feel collectively inside and part of
something entertaining, something that moves and stimulates,
that has variety, a business mix—a "collection of main things,"
Fullilove calls it: a city hall, a post office, a library, some recognizable monument, a movie theater, a toy store, restaurants, a deli, a
house of worship, an ice cream parlor, a coffee shop, a bookstore,
a bakery. "The point of all these attributes of the box," she thinks,
"is that we are inside something that is safe, interesting, and
rewarding. I'm not sure that the womb was interesting—maybe
it was at the time—but I do imagine that we are all born with a
memory of being enclosed." We need space that doesn't feel too
overcrowded or too undercrowded, where you're either jostled
aggressively or in a bleak openness without any definition.

Fullilove recalls meeting the poet Michael Lally one morning
in a café along Maplewood Avenue in Maplewood, New Jersey,
"a quintessential Main Street," she says, "with a movie theater,
supermarket, fish store, bookstore, toy store, three classes of
pizza, a take-out Chinese place, a Thai restaurant, a hamburger
place, an ice cream parlor, a jewelry store, a post office, and two
banks. You can get a lot done in a short amount of time." But
in 2015, the post office, once centrally positioned, relocated to
smaller premises at the end of the commercial core, opening up
its former site to private redevelopment.

Michael Lally said this is sad. Prices are going up in
Maplewood, and the people who moved there twenty years ago
will soon be shut out. Recent arrivals come from finance. "The
new building will be tall and we won't be able to see the blue sky
from where we are sitting." These larger-scale redevelopments
will alter the form of the street, the flow of people along the street,
the symbols on the street, and the kinds of people using the street.

The post office's use value has been shoved off to the periphery; in the core comes the rush of money; and the needs of people are threatened, "needs like blue sky that can be seen from the coffee shop window." "Blue-skying" might seem like something impractical—didn't Allen Ginsberg say that "lightning strikes in the blue sky"?—but it is part of the light, something vital for human well-being.

Why do the fortunes of Main Street always have to oscillate between being overbuilt or underbuilt, between priced-out or having no price at all? On the one hand, lively Main Streets become success stories. People come and love them, move into the neighborhood, and feel fine. But more people come than ever intended, and strange things happen, until Main Street looks overbuilt to old-timers, even though it feels okay to newcomers. Before long, there's too much investment and a once workaday street functions beyond workaday. Big chains step in, rents soar, and mom and pops and independents get driven out. The everyday chemistry alters. Main Street thrives yet loses its uniqueness, becomes less interesting than before, less diverse.

In a sense, that's the good news. The bad news is that other Main Streets turn into economic and cultural backwaters, suffer divestment, become dreary and depressing. Decline feeds off itself and turns into a downward spiral of avoidance and abandonment, a malaise where empty Main Streets are menacing Main Streets. Boom and bust are part and parcel of the same uneven, zero-sum development process. But can't there be some way to counteract opposite flanks?

At the end of *Main Street*, Fullilove pays homage to Sauk Centre, Minnesota, with its daddy Main Street of them all, the Main Street that Sinclair Lewis used for his 1920 novel *Main Street*. He'd called the town Gopher Prairie, an allegory of the narrowness of small-town USA. Lewis's protagonist is a young woman called

Carol Kennicott who dreams big and has radiant, cosmopolitan visions of how Main Street can become less dreary, less ingrown. But she marries, and her husband and the town end up pulling her back, keeping her in her place. "*Main Street* is a frustrating book," says Fullilove. "Carol is perfectly good and perfectly inept. She marries the wrong man, lives in the wrong place, fights with the wrong tools. Who wants to read 406 pages about that? Even the narrator is ambivalent, liking her one minute and impatient with her constant catastrophes the next. But the narrator's deeper impatience is with the status quo and its ability to suck the life out of good people who want to make things better."

It's hard to imagine life ever getting sucked out of Fullilove. During the launch, she read out passages from her book, and we got a flavor of its paean to the complexity and diversity of human life, to the beauty of it, but also the difficulties of it. While listening, I could visualize Fullilove strolling and scrolling through Main Street on a sunny Sunday afternoon, looking and hearing, interrogating the cityscape with compassionate embrace. For my bit, I suggested that if ever she needed a theme tune for these jaunts, and for her book, and for the best Main Streets everywhere, I'd like to propose Thelonious Monk's "Easy Street." It's a number that bobs along with the same playfulness, the same lyricism, the same dissonant chords and off-kilter rhythms as urban daily life itself and of Fullilove's evocations of this life.

That said, there'd be a little dialectical twist to the jaunt: Easy Street, for instance, is something of an *ideal* rather than a reality these days, a vision that's forever economically and politically constrained. Easy Street's sweet life won't come about easily. None of this, of course, is lost on Fullilove herself, who knows it well. Neither was it lost on Monk, our prophet of light. Indeed, we might recall that "Easy Street" appears on his album *Underground*, released in 1968, a year as racially fractious and fraught as our own times. The album's sleeve image has become as famous as the music inside—Monk at an upright piano, in his beat-up subterranean lair, coming on like Ralph Ellison's invisible man, a Black Panther resistance fighter and urban guerrilla glaring at the camera, telling us he's taking no more fascist shit. (Gil McKean's liner notes mention nothing about the music and focus solely on how "Capitaine Monk" took out a "honkie Kraut.")

It's quite probable, then, that for Main Street to become Easy Street, for love to trump hate, good people will need to engage in similar combat, in some kind of struggle and resistance, battling injustice and autocracy everywhere in our midst. Fullilove's vision of urbanism and society isn't only worth endorsing and cherishing but also something that will have to be struggled for. Thelonious Monk isn't a bad icon for any struggle, especially for any Black Lives Matter struggle. Yet, here again, there's another twist. For Monk's is an intricate music, and its healing power comes from a register that's peaceable and tender, gentle like the man himself (despite his mighty frame), like *Underground* itself, whose cover image bears scant resemblance to either the personality of the man or the music inside, where tracks like "Ugly Beauty"—another possible anthem for Main Street, USA?—are sweet and slow, hauntingly melancholy rather than explosively violent.

At the close of Fullilove's Zoom launch, Michael Lally took us into his own living room to share with us Monk's mood, focusing his computer camera on something hanging on the wall: a framed portrait of the musician himself, Boris Chaliapin's oil painting of Monk, which famously appeared on the front of *Time Magazine* (February 28, 1964) and now hangs in London's National Portrait Gallery. (*Time*'s feature on Monk was slated to run on November 29, 1963, but got bumped because of JFK's

assassination on November 22.) Lally told everybody how Monk was his hero, inspiration for his poetry, and how he'd excitingly acquired the issue at a New York newsstand, hot off the press over half a century ago. It had been his treasure ever since. Monk vibes soon resounded throughout the virtual airwaves; Easy Street struck up a chord on Main Street, alongside *Main Street*, and all of us, no matter where we were, suddenly felt what a great unifier the man and his music could be.

LALLY'S STORY GOT ME THINKING recently about another Monk legend, hailing from the same tumultuous year as *Underground*: an impromptu gig he did at Palo Alto High School in California. In October 1968, Monk's quartet was scheduled to do a two-week stint at San Francisco's Jazz Workshop. A sixteen-year-old jazz fan, Danny Scher, a Jewish kid and senior at Palo

Alto High School, a Monk fanatic, got wind and decided to call
Monk's manager Jules Colomby, inviting the pianist to perform
at a high school benefit. Monk wouldn't be far away, and Danny
could offer 500 bucks. Somehow, agreement was struck. Yet
would Monk really show?

Like the rest of the United States then, Palo Alto was gripped
by racial tensions. The city was mostly white and wealthy, while
nearby East Palo Alto was predominantly Black and poor, an
"unincorporated" area with no voting rights and soaring unemployment. East Palo Alto had begun a campaign to educate residents about Black culture and rename the city "Nairobi," after
the Kenyan capital. Scher said that wherever he saw a poster with
"Vote Yes to Nairobi," he'd paste his own ad for the Monk concert
beside it. "The police," he remembered, "would come up to me
and say, 'hey, kid. Hey, white boy, this isn't really a cool place for
you to be, given what's going on. You're going to get in trouble
here.'" Nobody thought it was true anyway, that Monk's quartet
would turn up. Tickets were priced at $2 and weren't selling well.

Danny's older brother, Les, had a car. He promised to go to
San Francisco and give the band a ride. On the day of the per-
formance, few were about the school. Until . . . until residents
and kids rubbed their eyes in disbelief as Les's car rolled up
with Larry Gales's bass sticking out the window, and he, Monk,
Charlie Rouse, and Ben Riley all getting out, strolling across the
playground in the rain. Suddenly, everybody wanted in, came
running over to the school hall, and for the next hour or so, before
an enthusiastic crowd, Monk brought a full house down, playing
brilliantly, the whole band blowing and swinging. For forty-seven
minutes, Black and white residents, young and old, parents and
grandparents, sat beside one another, overcame their differences,
and simply dug the music.

Incredibly, we can now hear how good the band was that

damp autumn afternoon in 1968. Fifty-two years on, a record-
ing was discovered, made by the school's Black janitor, whose
identity is still unknown. (He'd also tuned the piano for Monk.)
The quality is astounding and *Impulse!* released it on vinyl in late
2020: *MONK—PALO ALTO*. The album includes a reproduc-
tion of Scher's poster and the afternoon's program, accompanied
by a handsome booklet written by Monk's biographer, Robin D.
G. Kelley. It had been a magical Sunday afternoon. And nobody
cared that it poured outside. Maybe they didn't even care about
the referendum either, to change East Palo Alto to Nairobi, which
was soundly defeated nine days later at Municipal Council by a
margin of more than two to one. After all, they'd already seen
what an interracial gathering looked like, how it sounded, how it
could be solidified by music, by jazz.

Perhaps jazz can still be a solidifying event, can still transform
decaying and divided Main Streets into Easy Streets. On March
17, 2022, the *New York Times* reported on "Where Jazz Lives
Now," highlighting how "jazz bleeds outward" and how it is helping reenergize certain neighborhoods in New York, transforming
both venue and music, giving each a new edge in places once on
the edge. In the process, small businesses, especially independent ethnic restaurants, have been revitalized, bringing new life
back along neighborhood Main Street.

In COVID's wake, demand hasn't ebbed; some are even
saying a new scene is emerging and that "it's an uncommonly
exciting time for live jazz." New innovators in music are discovering new venues to perform, away from renowned landmarks like
the Village Vanguard and Blue Note. They're finding more mixed,
local audiences elsewhere, at less pricy haunts that don't look
like typical jazz clubs—in Haitian eateries and Afro-Caribbean
restaurants and bars, in Bushwick and Bedford-Stuyvesant, in
Crown Heights and Greenpoint, in Prospect Lefferts Gardens.

Crowds are "young, colorfully dressed patrons seated at tables and wrapped around the bar."

Here "are real blood-pumping moments," the *Times*'s article says, "where you can sense that other musicians are in the room listening for new tricks, and it feels like the script is still being written onstage." The music is improvised, like the venue itself, with new fusions and cross-pollinations between culture and technology, between digital music and place. Rooms are filling up, and the music sounds fresh. "It's really not about the money on Jazz Night," one restaurant owner says. "I think it's more about creating community and being able to create space for the musicians to do their thing and have a really good time."

7        Jazz

SOME DAYS, THE MUSIC SEEMS over for Main Street Great Britain and the Great British High Street. And when the music's over, in the immortal words of The Doors, "turn off the lights." British High Streets have had their lights turned off long ago. We've canceled our subscription to the resurrection. Few joyous sounds are heard. A stroll down the local High Street isn't so much a jaunt along Easy Street as a plunge into "Hard Times," something Dickensian, full of bleak houses. Indeed, COVID sealed the already precarious fate of High Street commerce. Long-range entropy turned into sudden catastrophe.

Store closures, boarded-up premises, dreary, disheveled streets, with dreary, disheveled people, worn down by life's hardships, strike as the order of the day. Under a typically gray British sky, everything becomes even more depressing, if that's possible. Those businesses still in business, like the ubiquitous array of High Street chains—Boots, W. H. Smiths

(surely *the* dreariest store in the land), Superdrug, etc., etc.—
hardly raise one's spirits. They're about as inspiring as a stick of
celery in a lonely field.

Well before COVID, the British High Street was on the rocks.
Yet after successive lockdowns, estimates reckon eleven thousand
stores have gone under, tipping a lot of High Street retailing over
the edge. Unit vacancies currently stand at around 16 percent.
Most of the casualties are chain outlets, unsurprising given that
for decades chains have colonized our High Streets everywhere.
They've monopolized and driven out smaller businesses. They've
been pretty much *all* the High Street commerce we've had. But
in killing off the competition, they overextended; now, they're
downsizing, leaving people with no alternative. Save thrift (charity) stores. Up to eighteen thousand more stores, restaurants, and
leisure outlets could fold as major retail groups like Debenhams,
Topshop, and Dorothy Perkins collapse. Meanwhile, Marks &
Spencer, with reported losses for 2020–2021 of more than £200
million, have axed over one hundred stores nationwide; more
closures are imminent.

House of Fraser (owner of Debenhams and Topshop) has also shut one hundred stores, including their London flagship at the iconic art deco building on Britain's prime High Street, Oxford Street. Billionaire Mike Ashley's Sports Direct bought House of Fraser in 2018 but has struggled ever since. According to one business commentator, "House of Fraser stores are drab, staff levels are low, and service terrible." It's pretty damning. Stores have failed to adapt to consumer demands, critics say, for both an in-house and online consumer experience. And now they're paying the price ("What Does the Closure of House of Fraser's London Flagship Mean for the UK High Street?" *Retail Gazette*, November 23, 2021).

Retail analysts reckon further troubles are in store for the British High Street. The challenge is how to reinvent it, how to make High Streets and city centers less reliant on chain retailing, maybe even less reliant on retailing *tout court*. In the meantime, the predictable and boring High Street we once knew is soon destined to become a whole lot worse: deserted, boarded-up, jobless. For decades, we've been in the grip of a Hobson's choice, between a sterile wilderness, on the one hand, or a dead wilderness, on the other. Alternatives have been throttled by market forces, by a lack of imagination and political will. Identikit Britain needs a new value system for its cities and towns.

GROWING UP IN LIVERPOOL IN the 1970s, I remember when you couldn't get a decent cup of coffee anywhere on the High Street. This was very troubling for me, a wannabe French surrealist shacked up in gloomy Garston. Those surrealists used to drink a lot of coffee. They liked to talk and hang out in cafés. And with all that caffeine inside them, afterward, they liked to walk the city streets. In those streets, they said, you could discover novelty and chance encounter. That's the meaning of life in the city, they said, novelty.

A little later, I read Jane Jacobs. Jacobs drank more gin than coffee. She particularly liked her local—New York's White Horse Tavern, along the same Greenwich Village Hudson Street block where she lived. Jacobs didn't much like what planners had done to cities on both sides of the Atlantic, nor what they were to mastermind. They peddled the silly idea that functional separation was the way forward, that spaces should have mono-uses—work here, residence there, leisure someplace else. Jacobs said this destroyed the mixed land uses and diversity that made neighborhoods vibrant, that brought life to cities of all shapes and sizes.

Decades on, weird things happened to our cities. Since Margaret Thatcher, we've not had much planning, even of the sort Jacobs dissed. The "free" market has decided things. And the free market soon discovered coffee. We have more places nowadays to drink coffee than the surrealist could have ever imagined. We knew something was up when Whitbread, the brewery group, started shutting its High Street pubs and diversified into coffee, supplying us with a Costa Coffee on every street corner—or on every other street corner, next to every Co-op, with a Starbucks and Caffè Nero close by. The surrealists can get their caffeine rush. But where, after supping, would they wander, seek out that novelty and fleeting delight?

Once the famine, lately the feast, an orgy of sameness. Steadily but surely, up and down the country, in that free market economy, our big cities and little towns have become alike. Predictable chain stores dominate, too ubiquitous to mention. When Whitbread acquired Costa in 1995 for £19 million, it had thirty-nine stores. When Whitbread went on to sell Costa to Coca-Cola in 2018 for £3.9 billion, there were thousands of stores—in fact, 2,700 as of 2021. Since the pandemic, Costa-Cola has slashed 1,650

CHAINS

jobs amid store closings and staffing purges nationwide—including forty-odd closures on mainland China. (I remember a few years ago flying to Australia, waving goodbye to a Costa at my Heathrow gate, only to be greeted by another Costa hours later, stepping off the plane in Dubai.)

Maybe it's just me, but there's something about the taste of chain store coffee; Costa's, like all the rest, has a sharp metallic bitterness about it, only ever tasting one way, irrespective of the store, irrespective of who makes it. Little wonder most people want to drown that bitterness with masses of milk and sugar or with frothy cream and chocolate, and Lord knows what else. I like to think coffee drinkers might opt for a less reassuring sterility of taste and place if given the choice. Perhaps it's too late. Perhaps they've already been conditioned into knowing only *that* taste. Which, of course, was the chains' principal objective in the first place.

I'm old enough to blame it on Thatcherism. Planning was bad, but no planning is worse. Let's be clear: it's not like there hasn't been any planning, more that our local authority planners have been bought off by those same big chains. They've had their pockets lined and political ambitions anointed. They've granted planning permission where they shouldn't have, given it for anything and to anybody who'll bring commerce to town, kowtowing to big chains most of all, offering them the kinds of tax breaks and rent holidays they'd never dare offer struggling independents.

Our local politicians and planners believe big chains are the most economically reliant and resilient. Famous last words. It's a warped understanding of monopolistic economics and of what a rich urban culture should be all about. Meanwhile, honest planners haven't been very imaginative or have given up too depressed. They should've read more French surrealism. And more Jane Jacobs. Nor has the free market been very free. Our cities are arenas for high yields only, for gleaning land rent, for making property pay any way it can. People are priced off the land. Only rich companies can afford to stay put. And then they leave.

SURREALISM HAS BEEN ON MY mind penning these words, because I've just visited a big exhibition at London's Tate Modern gallery: "Surrealism Beyond Borders." Many years ago, I swore I'd never go to another museum to see another Surrealist exhibit. I'd seen hundreds. They'd usually been curated pretentiously, smacking of pomposity and self-importance. They never captured the surrealism that I carried around in my head. Catalogs compiled by art critics invariably stressed fantastical juxtapositions and counter-hegemonic practices, liberational assemblages and strategies of defamiliarization—academic jargon destined for *Private Eye*'s "Pseud's Corner." Usually, too, these exhibitions of artworks by artists who hated conformism and predictability were colossally conformist and predictable, and such was the Tate's. Still, inexplicably, I went, somewhat predictably.

The exhibit, initially unveiled at New York's Metropolitan Museum of Art in late 2021, was vast, spanning eleven large rooms of the Bankside gallery, with paintings, drawings, photos, pamphlets, and films of surrealisms from around the globe, beyond a Paris-centric identity: from Osaka and Bogotá, Mexico City and Cairo, Haiti and Havana, Mozambique and Korea. Points of transnational convergence were highlighted, shared political allegiances; shared fears, too, about the state of the world, colonialism and war, exile and authoritarianism, civil rights and the plight of the creative artist in repressive societies. Those concerns never seem to die out entirely.

The collection was also keen to place greater emphasis on surrealist women artists, like Leonora Carrington, Kati Horna, Frida Kahlo, Françoise Sullivan, Dorothea Tanning, and Remedios

Varo; and on non-white males, like the voodoo-Afro-Cuban painter Wifredo Lam (with a Chinese father), and the American trumpeter, poet, painter, and Black Power activist Ted Joans, whose "Long Distance" exquisite corpse drawing game, produced over thirty years and pasted together from 132 collaborators on three continents, concertinas to over thirty-five feet in length, unfolding as almost the backbone of the whole exhibition. "Jazz is my religion," said Joans, "and surrealism my point of view."

While much of "*Surrealism Beyond Borders*" left me cold, typically dissatisfied, walking out the door, I knew, like other Surrealist exhibitions I'd seen, it didn't leave me with nothing: I'd had an *encounter* of sorts, getting me daydreaming about *something*. Besides all else, it made me think that those surrealist painters, photographers, and writers had much more interesting lives than ours, more experimental, more tumultuous lives; and they lived in more interesting places, more alive cities. I still dream of a piece of their action. But changing our way of seeing cities is more vital now than what changes our way of seeing a painting in an art gallery. The surrealists tried to make art-form a life-form. They drew on dreams and desire in conscious life. They wanted each to mutually inspire, to conspire as a new reality. The unconscious and conscious were to come together somehow, encounter one another and find a home in the city.

Encounter here meant more than mere meeting or rendezvous, more than a simple get-together; a complex get-together, perhaps, an interesting encounter, a contradictory, even conflictual encounter, an encounter that stimulates, that enlivens the senses, that teaches. That's what cities ought to be, surrealists said: sites of encounter, sites of "superior events," as Breton put it. That's how urban dwellers could prosper, feel more alive, be less bludgeoned by drudgery. Surrealists wanted people to inhabit a landscape of dream and desire, and Surrealism built this dream

house in the ashes of the dominant order, out of disgust and dis-
trust of this order, and so should we.

Surrealism rings out like a public payphone waiting to be
randomly picked up. Its call needs to be answered, its message
passed around; its sound needs to *resound*, to echo beyond the
museum walls. It needs to drift into the streets, onto the High
Street, where it's really meant to be. Surrealism needs to find a
voice again, become a soundscape, like a Ted Joans poem, played
to jazz, to Monk, or to a gravelly Archie Shepp horn. At the Tate,
one of the few highlights for me was watching Joans in action,
reading aloud to Shepp's tenor sax, in William Klein's film of
the 1969 Pan-African Cultural Festival in Algiers. Shepp, a self-
avowed communist (as well as poet and playwright), idolized
Charlie Parker before finding his own innovative voice in the
early 1960s playing with the legendary avant-garde pianist Cecil
Taylor. If only our cities could resemble in form and content the
lyrical atonal notes of tracks like "Lazy Afternoon."

The surrealists were wont to shock and exaggerate. André
Breton liked to invoke Lautréamont's exaggerated verse to
shock most. Breton loved Lautréamont's *Maldoror* (1869), a
poetic flight of fancy, the epic odyssey of Maldoror, "the prince
of darkness," whose bizarre hallucinations became Surrealist
touchstones: "the fortuitous encounter on a dissection table of a
sewing machine and an umbrella." Refrains like these, intending
to provoke outrage, reveled in encounters between absurd things
that were very hard for ordinary folk to get their heads around.
Yet the message was brought to earth later by Thomas Pynchon,
himself no stranger to the genre. Pynchon said he'd discovered
Surrealism in the 1950s and took from it "the simple idea that
you could combine inside the same frame elements not normally
found together to produce illogical and startling effects . . . but
any old combinations of details will not do."

*postmodernism*

*Situationist*

*chains re' London*

But the contrasts between the ideals of "*Surrealism Beyond Borders*" and the London cityscape are stark, and it's impossible to get that contrast inside the same frame. Exiting the Tate Modern that day, I crossed over the Thames on Norman Foster's Millennium Bridge (co-designed by sculptor Anthony Caro), intent on a Surrealist *dérive* around central London. (On opening day, in June 2000, Londoners nicknamed this structure the "Wobbly Bridge," as the slender ribbon of steel swayed alarmingly in the cross breeze blowing off the river.) Directly ahead is St. Paul's Cathedral. Passing along St. Paul's Churchyard, I'm headed west on Ludgate Hill. Already those chains are in abundance. There's Côte Brasserie (a higher-end faux French restaurant chain), Sports Direct, McDonald's (practically facing St. Paul's), and Wagamama (a fusion Asian food chain). Walking along, I'm greeted by Costa Coffee, Greggs (the dreadful British bakery chain, with two thousand outlets nationwide), and Pret à Manger.

Ludgate Hill is lined with "TO LET" signs on both sides of the street, flagging the ubiquity of office and retail vacancies. As I approach Farringdon Street, Leon (fast food chain) is on the corner, near Holland & Barrett (vitamin, nutrition supplement and health food chain). Over Farringdon Street, there's Marks & Spencer, more empty stores with "TO LET" signs, Boots, Sainsbury's Local, and then KFC. It's a motley array of sameness. No matter where you go, whether you're in central London or central Bury, these chain outlets are all absolutely the same everywhere: same store furniture, same colors, same layout, same menus, same décor, same shelf stock, same staff uniform, same smell, same feel, same same.

Turning right up Fetter Lane and another Holland & Barrett, with Pizza Express opposite. For a while, retailing disappears. Few people are about. The street is desolate. Fetter Lane becomes

New Fetter Lane, with office space on each side of the street, many new, sleek glass buildings. Their height, while medium rise, is too tall for the narrowness of the street, so everything feels enclosed. The space is dead. Defoe would have walked these same streets, as would his sympathetic, eccentric *flâneur*, H.F., as would Moll Flanders (Newgate Prison, after all, is just around the corner). Plague notwithstanding, these streets would have been more bustling then, more intensely alive, densely populated by people and dwellings, neighborhoods not yet emptied out by office space—by now redundant office space. These streets were coffined even when their offices were alive with occupants.

Now, there's around 58 million square feet of empty office space in London. Commercial property specialists suggest that with flexible work trends and remote working—the future long-term trend for around half of the UK workforce—unused commercial office space will continue to grow. Few businesses now want to commit to long-term leases; more than 60 percent of office space providers offer reduced rates or rent holidays. As of March 2022, weekly London office occupancy was 31 percent, compared with 63 percent pre-pandemic. Lights on, nobody at home. Soon, too, these lights will turn off. (Even so, with the prevalence of cranes in the City of London, offices are plainly still getting built and still, unbelievably, gaining planning approval.)

It's hard for pedestrians not to feel the disconnect here, the way Jean-Paul Sartre's protagonist Roquentin felt it in *Nausea*: a human being encountering cold, inanimate objects, objects everywhere around you, that tower over you, that provide the context of your life—objects you must live with yet are somehow cut off from you, beyond you, against you. They make you shudder with *that* feeling, the nausea that overcomes you, that alienated subjectivity. It's the landscape of money and finance, of High Street chains that enchain, that flatten life, that reduce much that surrounds us to a passive one-dimensionality. It brings on nausea. Or, rather, as Roquentin mused, "it *is* the Nausea. The Nausea isn't inside me," he said. "It is everywhere around me . . . It is I who am inside *it.*"

New Fetter Lane opens out onto High Holborn, and I turn left headed west, passing Wasabi (sushi chain), over Gray's Inn Road, encountering more office buildings, then Caffè Nero, another Greggs, and a (public) street sign with a McDonald's "M" on it, attached to a lamppost, giving directions to the said hamburger joint. Then Dorothy Perkins, Superdrug, another Boots, and another Leon; soon another McDonald's sign, similarly positioned on the public byway (how do they get away with it? Maybe because there's no mention of McDonald's by name, nor any image of their food), Blackwell's (chain bookstore), and another Pret à Manger. I cross the bottom of Red Lion Street, passing another Pizza Express. Just before Procter Street, I'm greeted by another Pret à Manger, hardly four hundred yards from the previous one. Crossing Procter Street, there's another Superdrug, another Caffè Nero, New Look (clothes chain) and another Costa Coffee on the corner of Kingsway, next to Holborn Tube Station, with another Wasabi on the other side of the street.

Over Kingsway comes another Sainsbury's Local and another sign for McDonald's. I decide to walk up Southampton Row, headed north now, passing a batch of vacant stores looking like they've been vacant since well before the pandemic. There's a lot of litter swirling about, and the landscape is worn and forlorn. I cross over Vernon Place, with another Sainsbury's Local to my left, and another Holland & Barratt to my right, then Ryman (stationary chain). Soon Taco Bell, facing which is another Costa Coffee and McDonald's. Russell Square appears immediately to my left, and after a little while, I turn right onto Bernard Street, encountering another Pret à Manger and Tesco Express, before joining the south end of Marchmont Street, opposite Russell Square Tube Station.

Now, in the heart of Bloomsbury, for the first time on a foot journey nearing three miles, things get more interesting. I head up Marchmont Street, with the Brunswick Centre on the right (a concrete, high-density, modernist housing structure built between 1965 and 1973), and the Marquis Cornwallis pub appearing to my left. Just afterward comes Marchmont Street's Post Office, lined outside by a large fruit and vegetable stall, my first glimpse of anything fresh. Immediately following it also my first glimpse of anything independent: "Bloomsbury Building Supplier," a locally owned hardware store and paint and plumbing supplier. It's been around here for thirty years, probably more. I know this because, in the mid-1990s, I lived around the corner, on Coram Street, and the hardware store was already well established then, frequented by me included. Not far away, on the other side of the street, is Alara Health Food and Organic Café, another independent and long-standing feature of the block. Ditto "Gay's the Word," an independent LGBT bookstore set up by a group of gay socialists in 1979, still miraculously hanging on.

There are other wonderful independent bookstores along Marchmont Street: SKOOB and Judd books, the latter being one of my all-time favorites, dear to my heart when this was my neighborhood. It's still run by the same two guys, now a lot grayer. SKOOB, nestled in the Brunswick Centre, fifty yards off Marchmont Street, is a more recent arrival. I remember it years ago at Sicilian Avenue, off Kingsway, and Judd Books was called "Judd Street Books 2" then, since the original Judd Street books was on nearby Judd Street, a little farther north, just south of King's Cross Station. That location always felt peripheral to me; the owners agreed, eventually amalgamating their stock in the

Marchmont Street premises, retaining the Judd Street name but later dropping "Street."

Marchmont Street was the London street I loved best. It was where I wanted to live, on it or nearby. It didn't only have bookstores and cafés; it also had an arts cinema, "The Renoir," still has it, in the Brunswick Centre, a stone's throw from my apartment. The neighborhood was my little utopia for a while. If anything, the changes taking place there over past decades, rather amazingly, have probably been for the better. The street hasn't lost its charm. Independents have been able to flourish, despite rising rents. I know this segment of London intimately, and it was always the intended terminus of my walk across town. I confess it, like the philosopher Louis Althusser "confessed" about his "reading" of Marx's *Das Kapital*, his "guilty" reading. He was no innocent reader, and neither am I, similarly reading central London's landscape with *intent*, like Althusser read Marx's landscape in *Kapital*, unpacking meaning, probing absences and presences, sights and oversights, the visible and the invisible. I could never be an innocent *flâneur*, a casual stroller through town, mimicking the casual reader strolling through a text. Instead, there's too much interrogation going on, too much critical investigation, so I confess my crime, my guilty reading, my partial eying of the cityscape around me.

Marchmont Street, for me, was the nearest thing in the United Kingdom that resembled anything Jane Jacobs evoked in *Death and Life of Great American Cities*. Here, I thought, were some of the inspiring qualities of her "intricate street ballet," ebbing and flowing in its "morning rituals," in its "heart-of-the-day" and "deep night" ballets. Marchmont Street likewise exhibited mixed-use diversity and clientele—young and old, students and bohemians, Asian kids and families, tourists and locals, yuppie professionals and poorer working classes, Blacks and whites,

gays and straights—out in public in a central London street. A
real rarity. A community center, a hardware store, a launderette,
a dry cleaner, a post office, a bakery, a dentist, a newsagent, three
hairdressers, a health food store, a Halal food store, two pubs, a
betting shop, several cafés (independents as well as a Costa), three
bookstores, a Waitrose supermarket (nearby in the Brunswick
Centre), a cinema, together with Chinese, French, and Indian
restaurants, all relatively happily sharing the space of one small
neighborhood block.

In bygone days, a café called Valencia served as my surrogate
living room. It's still around today, though with a bit of garish
makeover since my residency. I used to sit there for hours, up
on a stool overlooking a window, drinking coffee, losing myself,
trying to find myself, all the while watching the world go by outside. Inside, I felt a part of this outside action; detached from it,
anonymous, sufficiently absent, yet absolutely *present*. I surveyed
the crossroads, the junction with Tavistock Place, monitoring
things to the west and east, everything to the north; and, turning
around, I also could glimpse stuff to the south. I could see all
from this panoptic patch on planet earth. Sometimes, while I sat,
I thought I didn't have to go out into the world anymore because,
here, the world sort of came to me. I'd sip cappuccino, stare out
the window, listen to the radio, feel the pulse of neighborhood
life going about its daily round. I spent so much time there that
its owners—two Egyptian brothers—used to give *me* a present
every Christmas.

Those café days along Marchmont street convinced me that
the Surrealists and Jane Jacobs knew what they were talking
about when they talked about cities. One feature Jacobs insisted
upon was that cities need *hearts*. If we open our ears, we can hear
that heart beating, a human sound, like music. There's a natural
anatomy to urban hearts. Big cities usually have more than one

heart, just like they have more than one High Street, one Main Street. Yet always, these hearts will beat at busy pedestrian intersections. "Wherever they develop spontaneously," Jacobs said, hearts "are almost invariably consequences of two or more intersecting streets, well used by pedestrians." They'll have corner stores or corner cafés, corner pubs or corner public squares. Hearts thrive off diversity, not homogeneity. Rich people and rich businesses see city hearts as profitable financial investments, as organs to pump up and artificially inseminate. Under their watch, cities might look pregnant with possibility. But their real hearts have become sclerotic.

Nevertheless, on odd occasions, by some minor miracle or another, streets like Marchmont Street cling on to life, continue to have beating hearts. They retain diversity, manage to hold on to street spontaneity, to a certain kind of urban ambiguity. Things that shouldn't co-exist *do* co-exist. Perhaps it's no irony that one of our prophets of ambiguity, the poet and literary critic William Empson (1906–1984), twice opted to live along Marchmont Street: once between 1929 and 1931, and again between 1934 and 1936, at number 65, in a second-floor apartment now commemorated by a blue memorial plaque.

Empson's *Seven Types of Ambiguity,* published in 1930 when he was the tender age of twenty-four, was likely fine-tuned and finished off at his first Marchmont Street abode. The text has become a landmark in poetry criticism. Empson said the best poetry makes the best and subtlest uses of ambiguity, whether deliberate or subconscious. So should the best and subtlest urban planning and design. Maybe, then, we can conceive Empson's critical and creative treatise about poetry as a manifesto about the form and functioning of our cities. At its best, the city is a sort of poetic text, with the same rhymes and rhythms, ambivalences and ambiguities as those of the best literary refrains.

For many people, city life *is* ambiguity, a constant struggle between the realm of necessity and the realm of freedom, a balancing act between working and living, an active tension and perpetual contradiction. Marx devoted much attention to this ambiguity, to how the two collided in the socialist imagination, and how the Good Life involves liberation as well as livelihood. In Volume Three of *Kapital*, he says the realm of freedom begins only where the "mundane considerations" of necessity cease. Freedom begins, in other words, when basic needs for food and shelter are satisfied. A shortening of the working day, he says, is a prerequisite for making people freer and happier, for enabling ordinary folk to undertake more edifying activities that the world of work usually denies.

All kinds of aesthetic and creative endeavors might thereafter be released, even if it's just having more time to paste postage stamps in an album or chase butterflies in a field (which Breton loved to do at his home in St. Cirq Lapopie). Thus, *sensual stimulation*—pleasure, adventure, experiential novelty—is also a basic human need, Marx thinks, even though it's a category invariably commandeered by the idle rich, by the independently wealthy. Marx, however, insists that sensual stimulation is a right for *everyone*, not just for an entitled minority who buy or inherit their privileges, who monopolize them at the expense of everybody else.

Marx always held this ambiguity between freedom and necessity in creative tension. He seemed forever torn between a worker-ist, Promethean vision of life and an Orphean passion for play and pleasure. He tended to favor the former later in life and the latter in his youth. He knew, needless to say, that the two realms needed conjoining, that ethics and aesthetics had to co-exist. Yet he never quite figured out how to conjoin the two Marxes in his Marxism. Maybe for good reason: not only did he say he wasn't a Marxist, but he equally rejected utopian thought because it tended to favor one over the other: either a dour, closed, anti-human system or a self-realization based on "mere fun" and "mere amusement."

Marx never positioned himself in the center, never chose a compromise between freedom and necessity. Instead, he challenges us to imagine critical and radical forms of an Open Society, a society where people might work (necessarily, without surplus time) and be free, feel at once whole and more alive. He roots for a social and physical environment where the possibilities for human passion might heighten; where our senses—seeing, feeling, hearing, smelling, tasting, desiring, and loving (all Marx's words)—blossom as "organs of individuality" and "theoreticians in their immediate praxis."

Here the city comes into its own as a life form and life force, as a normative social space, where civic and cultural spaces, High Streets and backstreets, exist to promote and give scope to intense human experience and diverse human activity. In them, people might inhabit and participate in a more wholesome reality, a bit like a busy local farmers' market, where crowds congregate expectantly and the countryside encounters the city in all its ambivalence, like the fruit and veg being sold: misshapen, frequently dirty and battered, yet invariably flavorful and of high quality. Products are unalienated, just as direct engagement with producers is unalienated, just as the space itself expresses an honest clarity. Above all, everything *tastes*, and in our contemporary processed age, that's saying plenty. Items on sale are the kind of products dumped by big chain supermarkets, whose stocks are perfectly formed, mass-grown specimens, utterly devoid of dirt and flavor, like big chain cities.

A farmers' market isn't, of course, the only possible paradigm for wholesome urban space. Maybe another is the flea market,

something cherished by the Surrealists, especially by André Breton. Remember, early in *Nadja*, Breton wandering around Paris's great open-air *marché aux puces* at Saint-Ouen? He loved doing it every Sunday afternoon, he said, best of all with a friend. A little beyond what's now the Boulevard Périphérique, not far from the Porte de Clignancourt, Saint-Ouen's flea market has been around since the early 1870s, when ragpickers, clochards, and bric-à-brac dealers, deemed insalubrious by the bourgeois powers-that-be, were evicted from central Paris.

They soon installed themselves and their makeshift street bazaar in the northern periphery's no-man's-land zone and have been there ever since. The flea market thrived as a venue where Parisians could hunt down *trouvailles*, find antique oddities, upscale garbage, arcane wares (fossils, taxidermy, rusty old mechanical devices), as well as the occasional period treasure and artistic masterpiece—all at a price you could haggle over. For the surrealists, Saint-Ouen epitomized a site of the chance encounter with objects and people; surprises lurked around every corner and under each pile of junk. The surrealists would unearth here the artistic throwaways and ready-mades they'd make legendary.

In *Nadja*, Breton describes how, one Sunday, he and Marcel Noll visit Saint-Ouen. "I go there often," he says, "searching for objects that can be found nowhere else: old-fashioned, broken, useless, almost incomprehensible, really perverse objects in the sense I mean and love." At bazaars like Saint-Ouen, Breton says he delivers himself to chance, revels in circumstances "temporarily escaping my control," gaining entry "to an almost forbidden world of sudden parallels, petrifying coincidences, and reflexes peculiar to each individual, of harmonies struck as though on the piano, flashes of light that would make you see, really *see*."

Breton was a man who once gave one of life's great directives: "Expect all good to come from an urge to wander out ready to meet anything." In a beguiling passage in *Nadja*, he says, "I almost invariably go without specific purpose [to the boulevard Bonne-Nouvelle], without anything to induce me but this obscure clue: namely that *it* (?) will happen here." (The point of interrogation is Breton's own. What is the "*it*" in question? Who knows? Can anybody know? That's Breton's point.)

Several years later, in *Mad Love*, he recounts another trip to Saint-Ouen, this time with sculptor Alberto Giacometti, on "a lovely spring day in 1934." "This repetition of the setting," he qualifies, alluding to *Nadja*, "is excused by the constant and deep transformation of the place." There's enough novelty going on, Breton hints, that you'll never exhaust your visits, never walk through the same waters twice. Saint-Ouen is constantly changing, is the source of constant change, even to this day, and always there'll be "the intoxicating atmosphere of chance." "It is to the recreation of this particular state of mind," he puts it in *Mad Love*, in Giacometti's company, "that surrealism has always aspired." "Still today," says Breton, "I am only counting on what comes of my own openness, my eagerness to wander in search of everything, which, I am confident, keeps me in mysterious communication with other open beings, as if we were suddenly called to assemble." "Independent of what happens, or doesn't happen, it's the expectation that is magnificent."

In these passages, Breton touches on some of the grand themes of the Surrealist movement: an openness to novelty and chance; a celebration of adventure, of plunging into the unknown, somewhere unforeseen, impossible to anticipate in advance, someplace where an encounter happens—an "it," as he calls it. Meanwhile, the *expectation* of finding something, some new novelty or discovery, some *trouvaille*, is just as important as actually finding it, as realizing the expectation. And finally, for Breton, such above traits are distinctively *human traits*, putting us in "mysterious communication" with one another. We need this mysterious communication, and we're prepared to assemble around it. There's a generosity of spirit here, and one question we might ask ourselves now is: are we already picking up that ringing surrealist public payphone?

It probably sounds bizarre but maybe the thrift (charity) stores we've seen burgeon up and down the land, even before COVID, are the closest things we might encounter to the surrealist flea market. Don't they touch on the same sort of serendipitous experience? As businesses fold on the High Street—failed independents, runaway chains—thrift stores have moved in, occupying empty units, becoming a ubiquitous presence everywhere; a predictable external sight, perhaps, yet an internal adventure for everyone who crosses their threshold. Some people hate thrift stores: they smell musty, of body odor, and they're full of trash, and you never know who's worn those clothes.

Others, seemingly the majority of people, love them. Maybe because of our deep-down yearning for novelty, maybe it's that which is borne out in thrift stores? The human need to experience the unexpected? You're not sure what you might find in each visit, what shirt or blouse or jacket lurks on the rack, what record or DVD or used book, what household ware or piece of furniture; and at what price, something cheap, something designer, something you never thought you wanted and had no intention of ever going out to buy. And even if you find nothing, you've been stimulated, were expectant.

Indeed, you enter each store with a sense of expectation. A bit of adventure to the usual everyday mundanity. Of wanting to dig around stacks that don't resemble anything you'd find in a chain store. You already know what you might find there, in an environment that's anodyne and sterile, uniform and highly organized, programmed; that offers no real choice with its rows and rows of stuff piled high. No serendipity, no novelty, no surprise. Nothing is left to chance. The atmosphere is oppressive, the staff alienated.

Not so with the thrift store. A welcome antidote to the predictability and sterility of the High Street. A relief to pass time in a more friendly, relaxed, and informal ambiance, where people freely choose to be in, to work in. Besides, isn't it a good thing for the environment that those items are getting recycled, that there's less waste? And because thrift stores are registered charities, aren't they generally supporting a good non-profit cause, as are the people who shop there? Worlds removed from businesses answerable to shareholder greed.

But thrift stores are ambiguous, too. If they didn't exist, there'd be gaping holes along the High Street. Isn't that good? Yes and no. There are more than ten thousand thrift stores in the United

Kingdom; others seem to sprout every day, almost overnight. Charities receive mandatory 80 percent relief on business rates if their premises are "wholly and mainly" used for charitable purposes. In many instances, local authorities, keen to keep footfall on the High Street, desperate to fill vacant units, have topped up this relief to 100 percent, meaning big, rich multinational charities like Oxfam are exempt from paying business rates.

The little entrepreneur who wants to start up her café in the empty spot next door, though, won't get off as lightly and will be compelled to pay the market rent and the going business rate. That way, the proliferation of charities along the High Street guarantees market rents will never go down, even with an over-supply of retail rentals. Charities effectively mask capitalist failure without ever resolving the causes of this failure. And unlike an independent business that pays salaries to any employee, charities benefit from volunteer labor. They thus offer novelty on the High Street without ever offering paid work on the High Street.

Yet maybe the future of the High Street isn't about paid work anyway. Nor about conventional retailing, conditioned by the laws of exchange value. Maybe it's more about entertainment and leisure, about use value, novelty, and human encounter rather than strict monetary, financial encounter. Since COVID, some local authorities have balked at offering full rate relief to charities. There have been other appeals, too, to abolish rate relief entirely and get charities to cough up on business rates; it's a rebate that's effectively worth around £2 billion each year. (Even if the rate were only 50 percent, £1 billion might accrue for other uses, be put into a national fund that could support regional small businesses, especially in distressed areas.) Is there another urban strategy that might nurture thrifts alongside independent activities, like artisanal pop-up stores, temporary art galleries, and attic sale activities?

Can't the High Street be pedestrianized on certain days and hours to encourage more regular street markets and farmers' markets, pop-up events, and street dining? The pedestrianization of Soho, which shuts off its seventeen streets to vehicles between 5p.m. and 11p.m. to accommodate outdoor dining, offers a remarkable vision of a "hospitality recovery plan" (as Westminster City Council calls it). Sitting on chairs around tables from adjacent restaurants and cafés, Soho streets bustle with people. An amendment to dining laws, announced this year (2022) in the Queen's Speech, has made road closures and outdoor leisure a permanent feature of some of central London's neighboring High Streets.

Can't empty commercial units also be rezoned, converted into affordable housing, bringing people to live in town centers, at the same time as doing away with uniform opening hours, so that central spaces might be alive at all hours, not just at pub hours at night? Some independents might close after lunch and reopen later in the early evening, stay open late, a feature, for instance, of the smallest, most provincial French towns, which tend to come alive at evening time, when in Britain their counterparts are deserted and already dead. Mightn't we do away with uniformity altogether, ban chains (get bold!), instigate commercial rent control, and induce people to experience a more obscure clue: namely that it (?) will happen here; yes, happen even on *your* High Street?

Why can't central government empower local authorities to empower local, independent businesses? Real empowerment, I mean—empowerment of ideas. Many people, lacking money capital, have capital inside their heads awaiting realization. That's the alternative. That's the opportunity. Cities and small towns have lacked any sense of participatory democracy for a long while, and chains are a sure way to foster disempowerment in work and urban life. Our retreat to online shopping is merely a symptom of High Street alienation. Yet it isn't high-tech urban design that's at stake; more low-budget city acupuncture, of poking into urban tissuing meticulously and lovingly to enable sociability, finding new ways to recreate old stuff, like at the flea market—not rolling in roughshod with the bulldozer and a new Tesco superstore.

It's more about nurturing street space, developing floor space, reenergizing vacant units. The essential thing is to construct a human space in which experiential communication can be most effectively transmitted. Streets are *communicating vessels*, after all, capillary networks, where exterior and interior worlds constantly interchange and flow into each other. Physicality morphs into sociality, and vice versa. The more we stay passive objects, in a wilderness of sameness, of mono-space, the less we actively participate in the production of our own life, and the less we get out of this life. Could there ever be a sense that curious objects might induce curious people to one day create curious cities?

A WEIRD SURREALIST COINCIDENCE occurred the other night. Not long after I'd finished writing this chapter, I started reading in bed a Roberto Bolaño short story called "French Comedy of Horrors." It figured in a recent posthumous collection of tales from the Chilean scribe entitled *Cowboy Graves* (2021). "French Comedy of Horrors" centers around a ringing public payphone, ringing out one evening on a nameless lonely street in a nameless lonely town in French Guiana, picked up by a young lad and wannabe surrealist poet, Diodorus, who just happened to be passing by. The people on the other end somehow knew Diodorus would be passing by that night, by this particular payphone, and they knew that Diodorus was too much of a surrealist *not* to pick up the receiver.

On the other end is a mysterious caller who belongs to the "Clandestine Surrealist Group" (CSG), whom nobody has ever heard of, least of all Diodorus. But they're recruiting him into their secret group. They want him to come to Paris soon, to meet at rue de la Réunion near Père Lachaise cemetery. There are important surrealists still operative today, the caller says, doing vital work for the movement, living subterranean, subconsciously from mainstream life, in Paris's sewers.

The caller doesn't say, but CSG is following André Breton's edict just before he died (in 1966), that the time has come for Surrealism to go underground for a while to survive and prepare itself for future challenges. Breton says in *The Political Position of Surrealism* that he got this idea from Arthur Rimbaud. After the defeat of the Paris Commune, Rimbaud, a seventeen-year-old poet-protagonist, said the blood of its victims had drained away all hope for his generation. For a long time to come, Rimbaud said, truth will have to go underground.

Yet today, that ringing telephone, calling Diodorus to participate in the overground, is maybe one we need to answer ourselves. We need to let those unconscious possibilities surface again. We need to report for surrealist duty. But Bolaño says that, maybe, just maybe, no one will ever receive this call, that underground surrealists never existed, that poetic men and women have had their day, and that there is nobody around anymore to pick up the mysterious phone call even if it rang out. We no longer have ears for its frequency.

Something else surreal awaited me the same week I absorbed Bolaño's tale, which, incidentally, trails off, leaving us guessing about Diodorus's fate. (Did he get to Paris?) It was a piece in the *New York Times* called "Looking Back at the Payphone's New York Heyday" (May 27, 2022), a special requiem on New York City's public payphone, a poignant photo spread from the 1970s and 1980s, when the street payphone was in its heyday. Evocative images show how the payphone starred in the often-bizarre incidents and accidents of New York's daily life. Now, "these anachronistic pieces of public space" are being dismantled, about to be sidewalk history. They were once "little pockets of space" on the street, quite literally "communicating vessels" for voicing life's many dramas, vessels for communication now getting scrapped, a recognizable aspect of the city's life and landscape becoming little more than a memory.

They once helped find lost kids, mislaid wallets, and abandoned zoo animals. They were there for medical emergencies and acts of extortion. They were there for almost everything, guaranteeing that the city's private life had a distinctive public flavoring, rang out in public. During blackouts, power outages and fires, even though they were often vandalized, the public payphone came to everybody's rescue. (In 1984, New York's telephone company reported a sharp increase in vandalism after local calls rose from ten to twenty-five cents.)

And yet, there are no more payphones to ring out in public life. Surrealists must go elsewhere to listen for the sound of its underground, for other murmurs and ringtones in our age of cellular dialogue. You got to hope that we might take out those AirPods once in a while and open our ears occasionally to the outside world. You got to hope we might still be able to hear random sounds on the High Street, that our private selves can still become tuned-in public citizens.

8

NEW YORK HAS AN OFFICE SPACE problem, a glut. It also has a retail store problem: empty units standing out like missing teeth.

Those gaps are everywhere in town, especially in Manhattan, glaring cavities. In many cases, empty stores are directly related to empty offices. Workers no longer in the workplace spell shuttered up coffee shops, dry cleaners, lunch restaurants and bars, even newsstands—those small businesses that once served commuting office workers. New York's Comptroller's Office reckons vacant commercial premises across Manhattan have seen a sharp hike; in some parts of midtown, one in three retail spaces now lie fallow (see "Fewer Workers Planning to Return, Hurting Manhattan's Comeback," *New York Times*, April 12, 2022).

New York's mayor, ex-NYPD cop Eric Adams, has been pushing for a recovery plan based on thousands of workers returning to midtown and lower Manhattan offices. The city's 1.3 million private-sector office workforce, the mayor says, needs to get back to their desks. He wants crowds returning to central business districts, workers breakfasting, lunching, and dining there again, supporting small enterprises that will fast disappear without sustained patronage.

Adams's mantra, though, is falling on deaf corporate ears. Some of the city's biggest firms are urging employees otherwise.

Cheaper not to have offices

The management consultancy giant PwC told its forty-thousand-strong workforce it can now work remotely forever. Law firms and publishers like Penguin-Random House are following suit. Spotify has a seventeen-year lease on sixteen floors of 4 World Trade Center (at $2.8 million a month) but told its staff they can "live anywhere in the US." Facebook voiced likewise to its thousands of NYC employees, throwing into question what'll happen to their home at midtown's James A. Farley Building. The insurance company TIAA, Verizon, and many big techies (like Google) are all instigating hybrid working practices, insisting there's no compulsion to get back into the office. JPMorgan Chase, New York's largest private sector employer, said only half of its 271,000 employees would return to the office five days a week. So despite the mayor's pleas, in-person work presence looks like a blast from the past, not a glimmer of hope for the future.

The decline of Manhattan office workers is set to disrupt New York's collective life. For one thing, it threatens to undermine the city's real estate-reliant tax base. Overly reliant tax base, one might say. Offices: can't live with them, can't live without them.

Pre-COVID, office buildings in Manhattan supplied more than a quarter of New York's property tax revenue—money used to fund public schools, the police, parks, and public infrastructure. With 19 percent of Manhattan's office space available for lease, a near-record high, the dark days of the seventies' fiscal crisis loom.

Downtown, 21 percent of offices have no tenant. And without a regular stream of commuters, the region's mass transit systems will face even greater budget cuts, disproportionately harming those workers who still show up to work. Reduced funding means poorer service and crappier facilities. At the April 2022 Brooklyn subway shooting, recall that none of the station's CCTV cameras functioned. Rising subway crime will also present real and imagined obstacles to sustained usage, persuading many New Yorkers to think otherwise, if they can, about the daily commute.

And yet, while office occupancy dips, the city's residential property values and rents soar, somehow defying gravity. Vast swaths of the city's public life are destined soon to deteriorate, languish because of lack of funding; still, private sector rents rose 33 percent between January 2021 and January 2022; and in neighborhoods like Brooklyn's Williamsburg and Manhattan's

Upper West Side, 40 percent gains have been reported. (Average sales prices for Manhattan apartments jumped 12 percent during the first quarter of 2022.) This seems inexplicable, even obscene, while so much of the city still reels from COVID.

After offering discounts, landlords are beginning to turn the screw again. For tenants who stayed during the pandemic, the goodwill is over; for returnees, they'll have to pay even more than they did before they left. Property owners say they're trying to regain lost income and compensate for escalating costs of utilities and property taxes ("Rents are Roaring Back in New York City," *New York Times*, March 7, 2022). But hikes have only worsened the city's chronic affordability problem. Some fifty thousand people live in shelters; five thousand make do—or not—on the streets. Homeless encampments across the city have been aggressively dismantled by NYPD's Sanitation Department and Department of Homeless Services. The mayor is keen to highlight the "moral failings" of homelessness, clearing away the homeless for their own good.

Meanwhile, converting New York's seven hundred underutilized hotels into affordable housing encounters legal and technical barriers. A new $100 million fund to motivate developers to convert empty hotels into residences wallows because of regulatory red tape. Here, as with flexible work models, city policymakers have been slow off the mark, hardly grappling with what all this portends for the Big Apple's future. New York State has yet to relax zoning regulations, further hampering the conversion of office space into residential housing, including accommodation for low-income New Yorkers. So it goes.

I WALKED PAST KURT VONNEGUT'S OLD townhouse the other day, at East 48th Street, a narrow, white, three-story building,

mid-block between Second and Third Avenues. I was thinking about the expression he'd made famous in *Slaughterhouse
5*: "*So it goes*." Vonnegut said the Tralfamadorians uttered the
phrase each time they encountered a dead person. So would he,
Vonnegut said, in his novel. But I wasn't thinking so much about
corpses that day, about dead people, even though I could have
easily been—Russian shells, after all, were raining on Ukraine,
circa 2022, much like Allied firebombs had destroyed Dresden,
circa 1944. Instead, I was thinking about Vonnegut's expression
in conjunction with something I'd read in that morning's *New
York Times*, rolling my eyes because of the awful familiarity of
it: urban policy reverting to its old playbook of quack ideas. I'd
been hearing this stuff for decades. So it goes.

New York, like elsewhere in America—like everywhere in the
world—is handy at doling out huge amounts of public money to
line the pockets of an already immensely wealthy private sector.
Thus the *New York Times* was reporting on how Albany was soon
about to foot the bill for the Bills, for a new billion-dollar foot-
ball stadium in Buffalo, even as the Bills lost four straight Super
Bowls. Critics have damned this spectacular deal—costing New
York State $600 million and Buffalo's Erie County an additional
$250 million—as an egregious case of corporate welfare; fork-
ing out huge sums of public, taxpayer money to subsidize a team
owned by billionaires.

It's miraculous how the state finds ready money for private
services after crying poverty for public services. So it goes. Even
pro-capitalist economists wonder about the effects new mega-
projects like this have on civic bottom lines. "Large subsidies
commonly devoted to constructing professional sports venues,"
they say, "aren't justified as worthwhile public investments"
("Public Will Foot Most of $1.4 billion Cost for Stadium. Buffalo

Fans Cheer," *New York Times*, April 17, 2022). Much the same can be said about other mega-projects.

The most egregious of egregious mega-projects is New York City's Hudson Yards. This twelve-acre site, west of Penn Station and Madison Square Garden, had once been gritty rail tracks and storage yards for Long Island Rail Road trains. Completion isn't destined until 2024, yet much is already in place. Hooking up to the High Line and a revamped No. 7 subway station, Hudson Yards is meant to symbolize the pride and joy of a post-9/11 Big Apple, a celebration of Michael Bloomberg's mayoralty, his bleeding edge: New York, Inc.

Now, a $25 billion mega-plan brings shingled blue-glass skyscrapers, office space, deluxe condos, and high-end retailing galore, to say nothing of an eco-arts center and bizarre pedestrian walkway called the Vessel. Touted as Manhattan's Eiffel Tower, designed by Brit Thomas Heatherwick, the Vessel is a $200 million sixteen-story stairway to nowhere, resembling a truncated giant honeycomb. Nearby comes the "Shed," a $500 million eco-friendly arts center and performance space that looks like an aircraft hangar wrapped in a gray down comforter. In 2013, the City of New York handed more than $50 million towards the project to Related Companies and the Oxford Properties Group, representing the single biggest capital grant given that year.

But one of the most startling of Hudson Yards' scams, reputed to have amassed some $1.6 billion's worth of financing, is even more insidious, only quite recently becoming public news (see Kriston Capps, "The Hidden Horror of Hudson Yards Is How It Was Financed," *CityLab*, April 12, 2019). It centers on the controversial investor visa program EB-5, part of George Bush senior's immigration reform of the early 1990s. Bizarre as it may sound, the program lets immigrants secure visas in exchange for investment in the U.S. economy. We're talking here about super-rich foreigners who can pump between $500,000 and a million bucks into American real estate. That enables them—with no questions asked, no hoop-jumping—to gain fast-track visas for work or study. (It has been a favorite in pre-COVID years among wealthy Chinese families.) The monies are supposed to go into federally-targeted areas, into poor and distressed neighborhoods across America, so-called TEAs—Targeted Employment Areas.

The jurisdiction of TEAs—where its boundary lines are drawn—is rather loose, hence open to meddling and manipulation. And in New York, the Empire State Development, a public-private organization under New York State's banner, is the arch-meddler and manipulator. Somehow, it managed to secure Hudson Yards TEA status, stretching its remit into poor census tracks of Harlem. As such, funds intended for real estate aid in poverty-stricken neighborhoods like Harlem were siphoned off and redirected into a super-luxury mega-development. "Think of it as a form of creative financial gerrymandering," Kriston

Capps put it. That's how developer Related Companies raked in around $380 million at Hudson Yards, bypassing distressed area scrutiny through a greedy audacity that beggars belief. (And, by the way, the ex-president's son-in-law, Jared Kushner, had been busily promoting Kushner Companies' projects with EB-5 investors in China.) So it goes.

In New York's post-COVID workplace, "bleeding edge" takes on a different significance. Vampires have sucked blood dry. There's nothing left to bleed: empty offices and stores bereft of people characterize Hudson Yards, feeling a lot like the collapse of the dot-com sector in the aughts, highlighted in Thomas Pynchon's own *Bleeding Edge* (2013). Depopulated officescapes, unused cubicles in open-plan ghost spaces, gather dust. "Eerily deserted," said the *New York Times* ("How the Pandemic Left the $25 billion Hudson Yards Eerily Deserted," February 2, 2021). Kohn Pederson Fox Associates' one-hundred-floor pinnacle office and residential building at 30 Hudson Yards, taller than the Empire State Building, has around five hundred thousand square feet of unleased office space, casting a dark shadow across the shiny glitz. Hundreds of its condos remain unsold. With vast unpaid debts, which now include a $16 million claim for breaking its lease, retail anchor tenant Neiman Marcus recently filed for bankruptcy. At least four other upscale stores and several restaurants have likewise gone belly up.

When I strolled around Hudson Yards one lovely spring afternoon, the High Line was packed with people basking in the sunshine. Yet they were voting with their feet. Crowds thinned to a trickle inside the shopping mall. Listless shoppers aimlessly wandered a complex whose scale is so massively oversized. Everything felt alienating, unlived in, and dehumanized. Even the giant Whole Foods Market felt processed, supersized, starkly empty of organic humankind. Passivity prevailed in Hudson

Yards' rarefied air, both inside and out. In the chilly open-air shade, a small group of overseas tourists gathered at the base of the Vessel. They looked bored, puzzled why the structure was "temporarily" off-limits to visitors. Maybe they didn't know the Vessel's true claim to fame?

The Vessel first closed in January 2021, immediately after a 21-year-old man leaped to his death from its 150-foot spiral staircase. The previous December, a twenty-four-year-old Brooklyn woman had similarly jumped, following the death of a nineteen-year-old New Jersey man, an inaugural suicide, in February 2019. Witnesses then said there had been prolonged screaming as onlookers realized in horror what had happened. And just two months after the Vessel reopened, in May 2021, amid fanfare about a design overhaul to lessen the risk of suicides, a fourteen-year-old boy plunged to his death. Inexplicably, the height of the glass railings around the walkways, barely chest-high, hadn't been altered.

Police confirmed it as a fourth suicide. Initially "envisioned as a shared, immersive design experience," the Vessel's future now remains uncertain. It was meant to be Hudson Yards' quirky centerpiece, the brainchild of billionaire real estate developer Stephen M. Ross of Related Companies; instead, the Vessel may well be a tragic metaphor for our anxious age, when so many young people are deciding to end it all—and when so many other people have become so disgustingly rich.

One can only shudder at the public money squandered there, especially in a development so utterly banal, such a colossal white elephant. There's nothing at Hudson Yards to satisfy even a five-minute attention span. There's no intrigue, nothing that grips, no curiosity, no messy city life. Hudson Yards' banality resides in the predictability of its form and function, in its predictable sleek glass and steel architecture, catering for a predictable array of

financial and high-tech services, multinational corporations and accountancy firms, banks and management consultancies, high-end retail giants, each aimed at a predictable bunch of wealthy consumers. All real urban texturing and spontaneous novelty is expunged. So it goes. Meantime, will a $40 billion revitalized Penn Station—a mind-numbing 18.3-million-square-foot redevelopment, with ten super-tall skyscrapers and even more office space—move in the same egregious direction?

*Penn Station*

ONE OF MY FAVORITE NEW YORK pastimes, besides walking the city's streets, is sitting on the bench in front of Jackson Pollock's *Autumn Rhythm* at the Metropolitan Museum of Art. I must have done this, off and on, for nearly thirty years now. I've always thought *Autumn Rhythm* a rather marvelous painting, the product of Pollock's tremendously productive year of 1950; I've spent

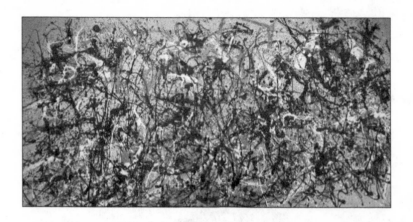

hours in front of it. Its black and white skeins and swirls, spirals and splatters, drips and dollops of paint, poured from Maxwell House coffee cans and spilled from wooden sticks, engulf the vast seventeen-foot by eight-foot brown canvas. (If you go up close, you can see other colors, like teal blue.)

*Autumn Rhythm* radiates an immense electrical charge, a kinetic energy that always seemed to me quintessentially urban, even though Pollock executed it on the floor of a small-town Long Island barn. The critic Clement Greenberg said this Pollock "action painting" represented "the crisis of the easel picture." All bets in modern art, Greenberg meant, were now summarily off. Here was something volatile, original, without a traditional beginning, middle, or end, breaking free of its borders, "painted" on the floor, stood on, danced around. With Pollock, it isn't perhaps so much what he meant in his paintings as what it means for you when you encounter them: all metaphorical and inspirational potential resides in the eye of the beholder. John Berger once said that Pollock's pictures appeared to be painted on the inside walls of his mind. What Berger left out is that they can leave an imprint on the inside walls of your mind as well.

For a long while, I've believed that a painting like *Autumn Rhythm* also represented the crisis of the classic framing of the city, wrenching us away from how, for instance, the Impressionists depicted Paris: with blurry, shifting brushstroke movement, yet with a movement always bound by a certain coherence, a certain pictorial ordering, a certain perspective of where the city centered and where it ended. Whereas with Pollock, this linear ordering is obliterated. Instead, he's letting us glimpse a deregulated sort of capitalism unleashed, whirring before you, with its spirals of capital sloshing around the globe, creating nodal points that gel as cities, as spaces like Hudson Yards, that flow into circuits of real estate development, into global money markets. Here, in short, is a graphic depiction of contemporary finance capitalism, its urban process in motion.

A decade or so ago, when the Occupy movement was taking hold across the globe, I had another idea about Pollock's imagery: that it was equally a representation of resistance, a pictorial depiction of the act of *fusion*, of people coming together, and that those great whirls and curves, puddles and dribbles, those wiggly threads of splattered black and white paint were actually points of convergence, nodal spaces that people occupied, that blazed new territories of possibility, all somehow connecting with one another. Indeed, Pollock illustrated nothing less than a radical geography of mass encounter.

Now, sitting in front of *Autumn Rhythm*, April 2022, in a quieter, more reflective mood, I had another thought about what Pollock might mean, something less explosive. Maybe it has to do with *autumn*, which oddly had never occurred to me before. When somebody once asked Pollock how he represented nature in his paintings, he famously responded, "*I am nature.*" Maybe, now, we can grasp autumn as implicit in the picture, as subliminally *there*, autumn as a season when things fall from trees, when mushrooms appear, when nature dies off, rots, only to nourish the earth as mulch for future growth.

The rethink was likely prompted by a memoir I was reading then by the Canadian forest ecologist Suzanne Simard: *Finding the Mother Tree: Discovering the Wisdom of the Forest* (2021). Simard has been thrilled by British Columbia's old-growth forests since she was a kid, when she foraged mushrooms and huckleberries, even taking to eating handfuls of dirt, relishing, like Gabriel García Márquez's Rebeca from *Hundred Years of Solitude*, the taste of damp raw earth. This taste never went away. Decades back, she noticed how commercial logging hacked down diverse old forests and replaced them with homogeneous plantations, stripping the soil of its underbrush. The logic went that without competitors and with more space for light and water, young saplings would thrive. But they didn't. Frequently they withered and died, proving more vulnerable to disease and climatic stress than trees in entangled ancient forests.

Simard discovered the reason lay in *mycorrhizal networks*, the threadlike fungi that envelop and fuse with trees. Here, beneath the ground, something amazing takes place. These fungi pass on to trees nutrients—phosphorous and nitrogen—and help extract the water required for photosynthesis. Around 90 percent of trees depend on these mysterious underground mycorrhizal networks—*mykes* is the Greek word for fungus and *rhiza* root—that link trees, even trees of different species, sharing life, knitting together the earth's soils in a complex system of symbiosis. When we see mushrooms sprouting, this is just one part of the story; only the fruiting body of fungi, its blossom, the visible realm where spores are produced and transmitted. A lot more of the action is subterranean, occurs deep down. Carbon, water, and nutrients pass from tree to tree via underground circuits, shifting resources between the oldest and the biggest to the youngest and smallest, from strongest to weakest.

Mycorrhizal networks are delicate gossamer webs of tiny threads, which, if we could dig underground, we'd not only see them as tissue stitching together much life on earth. We'd also glimpse an intricate fractal patterning resembling Jackson Pollock's *Autumn Rhythm*. We'd see the paint of his spirals and whirls, his nodes and synapses, as the constitutive ingredient of these mycorrhizal webs: the mystical and magical substance called *mycelium*. Mycelium operates more as a process than a thing, possessing an innate directional memory that spreads radially, forming a spidery circle of filaments in all directions, like Pollock's paint. If you teased apart the mycelium found in a teaspoon of soil, it might stretch to over a mile of thread.

Mycelium expands until it touches something, finds something to latch on to, to feed on and nourish, anything dead or alive, organic or inorganic, decaying and decomposing—not only tree roots and plants but old books and carpets, bits of wood and floorboards, trash and food waste, moldy wallpaper and even cigarette butts. (In Pollock's action canvas *Full Fathom Five* (1947), assorted moldy objects, like cigarette butts, actually get embedded in the paint.) Half-jokingly, Simard says these material filaments of mycelium constitute the "Wood Wide Web," nature's very own broadband, traversing humous subsoil everywhere. Channels for resource exchange and communication are always open, without tariff or subscription. In this other-worldly kingdom, the "internet of things" is nothing new: "smart" forests have been around for thousands of years.

While Simard says conflict in a forest is undeniable, she knows, too, that life abounds there because of negotiation and reciprocity, because of widespread mutuality. Earlier in her career, these

ideas were disparaged by her male "growth and yield" forest colleagues. Nowadays, Simard's vision of a forest ecology based on
cooperation and selflessness has begun to seep into the mainstream. Hers isn't so much a critique of Darwin, who, remember,
stressed contest and self-interest in the evolutionary process; it's
more a little caveat. When we think about sustaining life on earth,
fungi teach us that real resilience comes about through cooperation, not die-hard competition.

Loggers replacing diverse forests with homogeneous plantations sounds uncannily like the dynamics of today's urban environments, where developers similarly create homogeneous plantations out of messy old human woodland, hacking through the
city's old growth, disturbing well-established urban ecologies.
Stripped bare of human undersoil, devoid of selfless life, our
cities likewise wither from frailty. Only the richest survive in privately managed enclaves that exhibit little biodiversity. In these
new forest wildernesses, people are forced to compete with one
another, compete in labor markets, pit themselves against each
other in unaffordable housing markets. Our human mycorrhizal
networks have long ago been uprooted.

Mega-projects alter the metabolism of city life and, directly or
indirectly, kill off the city's old-growth forest. That forest probably required some sort of nourishment at the time; it was already
likely getting contaminated by invasive forest management. But
now it's gone, the city has less undergrowth than before, less
resilience, and is set to wither like the newly laid forests Simard
witnessed in commercial "fast-food" forestry. Trees depend on
their connection to the soil and one another—just like buildings
and humans. We, too, exist in a complex web of social relations
between ourselves and surrounding objects.

Demolishing and upscaling buildings severs this symbiosis
and disrupts the organic balance between people and people,

between people and buildings—between human space and physical space. In the social world, there are also mycorrhizal networks that help shape life. They offer support and cooperation, supply nutrients to people, especially to the weakest, and sustain the social structure of a shared soil. Fungi don't discriminate between species. They channel nutrients to multiple tree species. Theirs is a wondrous society of mutual aid. It prevails in the natural world, so why can't it also prevail in the human world? And why can't it prevail between different races and different kinds of human beings?

Maybe we need another program for urban forests, a city equivalent of Jean Giono's brilliant tree narrative, *The Man Who Planted Trees* (1953), about the French shepherd who, over four decades, disseminated hundreds of acorns, turning a Provençal wilderness into a wooded Garden of Eden. Giono's account was so compelling that many believed the selfless shepherd existed. Fictitious or otherwise, here was a man who cared about what surrounded him, a sort of public figure whose environmental management became a nurturing labor of love. His was a peasant's view of forest management, and perhaps we need a peasant's view of city management, too, like the peasant of Louis Aragon's *Paris Peasant* (1926). If only our developers and planners thought this way.

This surrealist classic—a "modern mythology," Aragon calls it—gives us similar ideas about forestry management, but its thicket is a dense city. It's a field manual about how we might treasure and preserve what we have in this forest before it's too late. Aragon's beloved arcade, the Passage de l'Opéra, was then about to be demolished to extend the Boulevard Haussmann, linking it seamlessly to the Boulevard Montmartre, creating the vehicular efficiency that the said Baron Haussmann reveled in and the Surrealists, as foot passengers, so loathed.

Aragon had often sauntered through the Passage de l'Opéra, under its glass canopy, tapping its hidden mysteries and charms. He delighted in the outmoded, in what you could find in the city's undergrowth, how you could stumble upon all kinds of secret lairs and earths, nests and rabbit holes; "a dark kingdom," Aragon says, "that the eyes of humans avoid because its landscape fails to flatter them." The peasant's Paris is a city full of trees and mossy old growth, constantly under assault. The city's "glowing woodland," he says, is perennially supplanted by commercial forestry, destroying much quirky, eccentric shrub life nestled within it.

The peasant is born on the land, is of the land, lives off the land. Only in this case, it's the city landscape we're talking about, how we might cultivate an urban garden, one belonging to the whole community; how we might collectively sustain this "enchanted forest," how we might dig away at it, manage it, renew it, without destroying its spell. Aragon wants us to cultivate this garden like a poet might conceive a poem, an everyday poem, like an ordinary stroll down Main Street, humming to yourself. The life of Aragon's peasant is hauntingly poetic, full of dreams. But while the peasant's dream is poetic, it isn't idealist. Nor is it abstractly philosophical. Peasants tend not to think in terms of abstractions. Their world is practical and concrete. They pragmatically labor the land and doggedly struggle for survival.

And that's how we need to cultivate our urban policy, how we need to doggedly foster our mycorrhizal networks, our relationship between buildings and streets—the complex ecosystem that constitutes our public realm. This is our shared forest, the surroundings that form our habitat, the one we work on and work with, the one we make and frequently break. Maybe someday we'll dream the peasant's dream, the dream of a harvest moon, when cooperative roots push up and nourish the earth and ripen into gorgeous fruits and crops. Over eons, through symbiosis and coevolution, our natural forests have grown tall. They were once small, puny, yet developed over time into a collective form of life that is mighty and magnanimous. Can we ever imagine our urban history rising to such luminous heights? Could we ever imagine a peasant dreaming of such towering office space?

9

ONE OF THE GREATEST URBAN wanderers was James Joyce's Leopold Bloom from *Ulysses* (1922). I know, I know, you're going to say, hang on a minute, isn't Bloom fictional, a purely literary invention, a character of one of our greatest twentieth-century writers? It's true, Bloom isn't real, wasn't real. Yet he can become real for us even if he's make-believe. He can become a character who's alive, whom we bring alive, make believe is true, as much a role model in our times as he was for Joyce in his.

*Ulysses* is a marvelous street book, taking us right into "the heart of the Hibernian metropolis." And though a lot of the "action"—if we can call it "action"—is internal, a dialogue inside the heads of protagonists, it's noteworthy how much of this takes place in *public*. It's almost as if the inner life of people, as they roam the city, going about their daily business, is released by being out in public, that the outer life somehow nourishes the inner life, and vice versa. Being in public heightens the inner world, stimulates it.

Joyce's protagonist Bloom is the direct dialectical counterpart of his most famous peer, Marcel Proust's alter-ego Marcel, whose consciousness of the outside, of the public world, heightens the more he spends indoors, alone in his bedroom, within four very private walls. At the beginning of *The Prisoner* (the fifth volume of *In Search of Lost Time*), dozing in bed, Marcel perceives from the early morning light and from the first street noises what kind of day it is—"whether sounds reached me muffled and distorted by dampness or twanging like arrows in the empty, resonant space of a wide-open morning, icy and pure." "It was, in fact," he says, "mainly from my bedroom that I perceived the world around me."

While Marcel lies in bed, Bloom is out bright and early, roaming a little after 8 a.m. in search of his breakfast, a pork kidney from Dlugacz's butcher's store. Bloom's day is already unfolding in all its unadulterated ordinariness, on a mild June Thursday morning, passed almost entirely outdoors, in the public or quasi-public realm—at a cemetery, in a public library, in a maternity hospital, at the open offices of a newspaper, on a beach promenade, in a cabman's shelter, in assorted bars and restaurant, as well as out on Dublin's streets, encountering people likewise going about their daily rounds. In the streets, Bloom muses, "life is a stream," "always flowing in a stream, never the same."

For Joyce, Bloom was an anti-hero Everyman, an Odysseus-like character; and a day in the life of this Jewish Dubliner, a progressive man, with cosmopolitan leanings, an outsider in a provincial land, is very much as *epic* as any Greek drama. Richard Ellmann, Joyce's renowned biographer, put it pithily: "Joyce was the first to endow an urban man of no importance with heroic consequence." For Joyce, everyday life in the street isn't simply an adventure, as the surrealists had it; it can also have Homeric qualities, be the very basis of world history, the starting point of what is possible and impossible in life. Above all, it *is* life. There's nothing other than the everyday, epic even when little happens.

Joyce exposes everyday urban life in all its ambiguities—in its baseness and joys, in its poverty and fecundity, in its fumbling myopia and sometimes clear-sighted grandeur. *Ulysses* is thus the antithesis of traditional novels, of those that present a plot with a hero, recounting his progress and dramatic rise up the pecking order, his towering emergence on the world stage, overcoming all and everyone. Bloom's reality, by contrast, is overwhelming in its triviality and occurs low-down. His only loftiness is the decency and decorum of his street encounters. They reveal an admirable humility that few great heroes ever have. Bloom demonstrates dignity in his daily affairs, how he greets people in the street, urging himself to make eye contact, how he shows respect and curiosity, sympathy and kindness about the plight of other Dublin citizens who've hit hard times, who suffer woes—like the pregnant Mina Purefoy, three days in agonizing labor. "It would simply kill me," Bloom says.

People used to ask Joyce: "Who is Bloom?" "A good man," he said, "a worldly man," despite never going anywhere. "He's a cultured allroundman, Bloom is," says the character Lenehan in *Ulysses*. "He's not one of your common of garden . . . you know ... There's a touch of the artist about old Bloom." Indeed, Bloom straddles the dialectic between artist and citizen, autodidact intellectual and common man, a bumbling ad-canvasser (his day job) and humble democrat.

Wandering around Dublin, flowing through its buildings and people, its human traffic, its sights and smells, through the sheer variety and vitality of its voices, Bloom's story might be our story: how to avoid crashing into rocks, getting washed away by the tide; how to navigate oneself through life's many pitfalls and human hazards. (At one point in *Ulysses*, someone discovers the perils on the sidewalk of a banana skin: "Fellow might damn easy get a nasty fall there coming along tight in the dark.") It's like Odysseus directing his ship, having his oarsmen pull away from those wandering rocks, from the whirlpools of the great human ocean. Bloom's archipelago is Dublin, and we can follow his trials and tribulations as we steer ourselves through our own urban archipelago.

"Wandering Rocks" is a special episode of Joyce's single-day epic, a staccato set-piece where Bloom mixes himself in the flow of the street and with the citizens of the land. Its eighteen short, fleeting scenes represent a brilliant urban montage, a panned glimpse of things happening, synchronically and diachronically, between three and four o'clock. We can encounter, in motion, a good chunk of the cast of *Ulysses*: the Jesuit priest Father John Conmee, a blind piano tuner and Italian tutor, Stephen Dedalus and father Simon, daughters Katey, Boody, Maggie, and Dilly, Bloom's cronies and enemies like Blazes Boylan (copping off with Molly, Bloom's wife, during this very hour), Martin Cunningham and Corny Kelleher, Ned Lambert and Miss Dunne, Fanny M'Coy and C. P. M'Coy, Buck Mulligan and Tom Rochford, J. J. Molloy and many more, all cameoing as the viceroy's cavalcade wends its way across Dublin.

It's a motley microcosm of a galaxy most city denizens would recognize as their own, the breadth and breath of city life laid bare. Unassuming as he is, Bloom dominates. He's ever-present even when absent, a man dressed in black never far away, about to step out from around the corner, ebbing and flowing with the tide, coming and going in the text as he comes and goes on the street. His flow follows the Liffey's flow, coursing through the city. On the move, Bloom spots the same "throwaway" leaflet, announcing "Elijah is Coming," bobbing up and down in the river, which he'd seen hours earlier, tossed into the street, as his day began: "a crumpled throwaway rode lightly down the Liffey, under Loopline bridge, shooting the rapids where water chafed around the bridgepiers, sailing eastward past hulls and anchorchains, between the Customhouse old dock and George's quay."

There's something fascinating about how Joyce constructs not only *Ulysses* but also how he creates Bloom. It involves a notion that crops up a few times explicitly in the text, offering a clue to Joyce's whole method and intent: the concept of *parallax*. Around lunchtime, in the episode "Lestrygonians" (a tribe of man-eating giants in Homer's *Odyssey*), food is very much on Bloom's mind. And in his pursuit for bodily nourishment, for food for thought, for feeding the brain, he mentions parallax passing the "timeball" at Aston Quay, recalling how Dunsink Observatory is twenty-five minutes behind Greenwich Mean Time—on account of the sun, seen in two different places by each observatory at the same time. This is parallax: how different lines of sight afford slightly different views of an object.

Bloom says he never really understood parallax—despite having Sir Robert Ball's "fascinating little book," *The Story of the Heavens* (1886), in a blue cloth edition, on his living room bookshelf. Yet Bloom's ruminations indicate he gets Ball's point more than he maybe thinks, internalizing it as his own personal sensibility. "Let us take a simple illustration," says Ball. "Stand near a window whence you can look at buildings, or the trees, the clouds, or any distant objects. Place on the glass a thin strip of paper vertically in the middle of one of the planes. Close the right eye and note with the left eye the position of the strip of paper relative to the objects in the background. Then, while still remaining in the same position, close the left eye and again observe the position of the strip of paper with the right eye. You will find that the position of the paper on the background has changed."

But parallax for Bloom, as for Joyce, can be interpreted somewhat differently from a celestial understanding. For one thing, Bloomsday—Thursday, June 16, 1904—might best be described as one twenty-four-hour "parallactic drift." Indeed, one could push it further and say that Joyce makes Bloom a purveyor of parallax: he sees things, often the same thing, from different vantage points—*"but don't you see? and but on the other hand,"* Pisser Burke mimics Bloom, ridiculing his ability to see an issue from differing angles, for grasping a problem in its deeper, all-round complexity.

A major stumbling block for "reading" *Ulysses* is precisely following Joyce's parallax shifts, his sudden jolts in perspective, his and Bloom's "parallactic drifts" throughout the day. Shifts in sentences frequently signal shifts in parallax, movements from a first-person "I," as an internal monologue, to a third-person "he" or "she," voiced by an exterior narrator; a movement between the subjective self and a commentator looking on, somebody who's narrating the action objectively, from a position outside the self. This is why *Ulysses* can be appreciated orally, hearing it performed, enacted by different readers, since the shifts in parallax then get articulated by recognizably different human voices, and we can follow the streams of thought as well as the streams of action. One of the great feats of the Bloomian parallactic drift is perhaps one of the greatest takeaways from *Ulysses*: Bloom's ability to think and see as a *public* and *individual* at the same time, as both an "I" and a "we," from his own and another's perspective.

The "we" in question here is the *demos*, the public at large. The Bloomian "I" is thus also the Bloomian "we," we, the people—at least, we, the progressive people. Such a "binocular" vision likewise keeps a hold of the ambiguity between the realm of freedom and the realm of necessity. As a secular Jew, Bloom sees the sanctity of individual rights yet understands the collective duties of a responsible citizen. Vitally, he has an openness and awareness to both at the same time. His isn't a desire to impose one over the other, to assert a singular selfishness or crushing authoritarianism. Bloom is a citizen of the city and a citizen of the world, not a blinkered bigot. He's someone who sees the reality of life and history very differently from, say, Joyce's character "the citizen," who figures in "Cyclops," *Ulysses*'s most explicitly political episode, a drama unfolding in the early evening in Barney Kiernan's pub.

No coincidence that the Cyclops is a one-eyed giant, a troglodyte brute, monocular in outlook. Bloom, on the hunt for Martin Cunningham, enters the Cyclops's den at Barney Kiernan's and soon gets lured into banter about politics. Before long, he encounters the menacing jingoism of this "citizen," a bullying Irish nationalist, sitting in the corner, in his "gloryhole," having "a great confab," frothing at the mouth like his mangy mongrel beside him. His ultra-nationalist discourse is obsessively single-minded, blind to all other problems of Ireland; a pseudo-populist rhetoric not out of place in today's mainstream, sounding like a rampant Brexiteer or Trumpite, a one-eyed Cyclops about to storm the Capitol, waving the "Make America Great" flag, even bearing an uncanny resemblance to a red-necked Proud Boy: "broadshouldered deepchested stronglimbed redhaired freelyfreckled shaggybearded widemouthed largenosed long-headed deepvoiced barekneed brawnyhanded hairylegged rud-dyfaced sinewyarmed hero."

As the drinks flow, the conversation turns heated, becomes visceral, and the citizen and his cronies mock the abstemious Bloom, begrudging his broad-minded internationalism and Jewishness, his preaching of universal love: "I mean the opposite of hatred," he stammers, aware of being on hostile turf. Martin Cunningham, who, earlier in the morning at Paddy Dignam's funeral, Bloom considered a "sympathetic human man . . . intelligent," turns out to be a closet Jew-hater, siding with the citizen and his clan. "Persecution," responds Bloom, gently, "all the history of the world is full of it. Perpetuating hatred among nations." (Bloom's hostile encounter here isn't too dissimilar to that of Proust's man of the world, Charles Swann, Bloom's upper-class Jewish *semblable* and *frère*, when he too is denounced by anti-Semites and anti-Dreyfusards like the Duc de Guermantes.)

"Strangers," says the citizen. "Our own fault. We let them come in. We brought them in. The adulteress and the paramour brought the Saxon robbers here." "What is your nation if I may ask?" the citizen grills Bloom. "Ireland," Bloom says. "I was born here. Ireland." "The citizen," writes Joyce, "said nothing only cleared the spit out of his handkerchief to swab himself dry." "And I belong to a race too," says Bloom, after a minute's reflection, standing his ground, "that is hated and persecuted. Also now. This very moment. This very instant."

"Are you talking about the new Jerusalem?" says the citizen. "I'm talking about injustice," says Bloom. One of the citizen's associates, John Wyse, butts in, "stand up to it then with force like men. . . . Mark for a softnosed bullet." "But it's no use," says Bloom. "Force, hatred, history, all that. That's not life for men and women, insult and hatred." For a while, Bloom exits but then

returns, reminding the gloryhole of the richness and cosmopoli-
tanism of Jewish intellectual culture: "Mendelssohn was a jew
and Karl Marx and Mercadante and Spinoza. And the saviour
was a jew."

"By Jesus," raves the citizen, upon hearing this, "I'll brain that
bloody jewman for using the holy name. By Jesus, I'll crucify him
so I will. Give us that biscuitbox." And here Joyce winds up his
one-eyed episode, with the rabid citizen chasing after Bloom,
who's bidding a hasty retreat, and the citizen hurling the old tin
box at him outside on the street, with all hell breaking loose and a
Dublin populace shouting and laughing and Bloom leaping into
a jarvey cab to save his life and "the bloody mongrel after it with
his lugs back for all he was bloody well worth to tear him limb
from limb."

WHAT CAN WE MAKE OF Bloom fleeing the Cyclops? Was he
wimping out, or had he already made his point, doing so without violence? In a sense, Bloom didn't back down, didn't ignore
the slights made against him; he only avoided getting drawn into
a physical confrontation. The latter, of course, informs much of
our own bitterly divided political landscape. Assorted Cyclops
seem to set the political agenda almost everywhere, deliberately
provoking violent confrontation and serial blindness. We saw this
coming in a pub like Barney Kiernan's, a dreary drunken breeding
ground for xenophobia and chauvinism, populated by rather sad,
alienated, angry men, a microcosm of today's rather unfortunate
macrocosm. Bloom's parallactic drifts and calm practice of parallax prove a useful antithesis of this, for envisioning life through
binocular lenses, engaging with bigots without stooping to the
low level of bigots. And while he's moderate in temperament, his
politics aren't moderate, no way limp and pitched lamely in the

middle. He's no faint-hearted liberal. Instead, Bloom is a socialist who wants "the reform of municipal morals." "No more patriotism of barspongers," he says, "and dropsical impostors."

He's a patient pacifist, a disliker of injustice and hypocrisy, who enters into relations with other people with a sense of equality, concerned about what happens beyond his doorstep. It's a sensibility perhaps best described as *pre-neoliberal*. Bloom's ability to see both the wood and the trees lends itself to an intelligence universally lacking at present; a non-violent, democratic yearning that can inspire a Left at a time when many of its protests have been cornered, when nearly everything once considered desirable for ordinary working class and déclassé middle-class people—Joyce's own constituency—all the stuff that once seemed to belong to the working classes, has now been claimed or bargained away by the Right, by the rightward monocular drift of the current state of the world.

And our cities, too, have fallen, have become crestfallen, with their public spirit ripped apart, crushed beneath this reactionary sway. Cities were formerly thought to be progressive enclaves; now, you can't be so sure. Citizens have been taken in by *the citizens*, by one-eyed monsters, by the Trumps, Johnsons, Bolsonaros, Dutertes, Modis, Orbans, and Putins of our age, who've turned their subjects into one-eyed monsters themselves. Suddenly, people have been taken in by the mood music of demagogues and autocrats, whose theme tunes top the charts. Meanwhile, rights—including the right to the city, once the cry and demand of progressives, the right to affordable housing, the right to justice, etc., etc.—now get overwhelmed by the right to life and right to bear arms, by the right to personal liberty and not to wear a face mask, not to be vaccinated, the right to be greedy and selfish and not give a shit about anybody else. That's *my* right, right?

It's the right to do anything you want, any way you want, to insult and maim, to do it all under the banner of the right to free speech. It also apparently means the right to lie, to peddle false news and false claims (the election was rigged, and so on). One time, too, direct action on the streets was enshrined in left-wing politics; now, it's the Right who're trying to reclaim the streets, who mobilize outside the state capitols, who march downtown, who storm the Capitol, who proclaim *their* right to direct democracy, throwing more than biscuit tins. It's a world gone viscerally topsy-turvy. Bloom would have had none of it.

That's why we might see him as a much-needed public figure, as a walking advocate of the *social contract*; his tempering of a general abrasive will is a gentle reminder about our duties toward one another. It's to remember, as Rousseau remembered, that rights as citizens without the duties as subjects is the ruination of the body politic. We've been ruined for a while now. In many ways, Bloom incarnates Rousseau's conception of *political society*, where rights make one aware less of what belongs to others than what doesn't belong to oneself. It's to reorientate the focus, to shift parallax, to make urban life whole again, to bring the private and the public together, freedom with necessity.

Bloom accepts the "reciprocal commitment" that Rousseau suggests any civilized culture needs between society and the individual. Each person finds themselves doubly responsible, having an obligation to themselves and society writ large. It's a reciprocity that functions best through a parallactic understanding of life, of oneself and society, of how the private "I" must also sometimes shift into the public "we." What Rousseau calls the public person assumes a role of a conduit, acts as a sort of human Higgs Boson, where city matter and city matters gel together through bundles of public particles, through people like Bloom, who busy themselves becoming points of articulation between private and public realms, ensuring that both cohere, co-exist in relative harmony, without each shattering apart as anti-matter.

The great urbanist Jane Jacobs hinted at the need for such public people in the city. She labels them "public characters," and her famous resuscitation of dead American cities is unsurprisingly full of them. A public character, Jacobs says, a chip off Joyce's block, needs no special talent or wisdom to fulfill their function, although often they do. They just need to be present, have frequent contact with "a wide circle of people." Their main qualification is that they *are* public, that they talk to lots of different characters, so that "news travels that is of sidewalk interest." Bloom could be seen as a perfect example of a public character, a roving presence on the sidewalk, an observer and participant, a critic and an integrator, a cultivator of contact and encounter.

Jacobs points to public characters such as doormen and waiters, barkeeps and storekeepers who look out for what's going on in the street and in the neighborhood, for what's happening to businesses on the block, on Main Street and on the High Street. These public characters cement together the interior with the exterior, the semi-public domain of a bar or a pub or a store, with the outside world beyond, on the street. Importantly, the best semi-public spaces here demonstrate a porosity between the private and the public, a seamlessness where you can be private in public and public in private; and it's the public characters that can make this worthwhile, make the seamlessness inviting, welcoming. They're open to the outside, just as the inside comes alive with the cast of the outside, with its diverse public. These spaces, in turn, usually become animators of and anchor points for the High Street and Main Street, drawing people in who want to stick around. We might remember how much of Joyce's writings feature publicans, barkeeps, and pub owners, folk like H. C. Earwicker, protagonist and star of *Finnegans Wake*, the great dreaming "innholder, upholder," who runs the Mullingar Inn in Chapelizod, a Dublin suburb.

Jacobs assumes that most public characters, because of the idea embodied in their identity, that is, *public*, are progressive people, open to the outside world even as they care—especially as they care—about their immediate locale. But there are bars like Barney Kiernan's that seem off-limits to a public, that aren't run by public characters—or are run by what Jacobs sees as the *wrong* public characters since they're not soliciting a more inclusive clientele, but foster *anti*-public sentiment, a mistrustful world, not welcoming everyone and anyone. Rather, they are spaces where minorities like Bloom feel out of place, unwelcome, instinctively ill at ease. He could sense the heaviness in the air.

Earlier in the day, at lunchtime, Bloom had entered another Dublin public house, Davy Bryne's, where the atmosphere felt convivial, more publicly inviting and homely. Bloom named it a "*moral pub*." One of the things that Bloom likes about Davy Bryne's is that Davy himself is a more compassionate character who "doesn't chat." He doesn't judge people or bad-mouth them in secret. "Stands a drink now and then," Bloom says. "But in leapyear one and four." "Cashed a cheque for me once," says Bloom. He doesn't bet on horses, either, and is a presence in his bar without being obtrusive or invasive. He says he knows Bloom "well to see." "He's a safe man, I'd say," says Davy Byrne of Bloom, like Davy himself. The establishment has its regulars, to be sure, perched up on their pews, in their nooks, like Nosey Flynn in one corner; but these are benign drinkers, harmless despite having their ears open for gossip. "Hello, Bloom." "Hello, Flynn." "How's things?" "Tiptop . . ." Bloom feels comfortable enough to linger, to take a restorative glass of Burgundy and a Gorgonzola sandwich. "Stopgap. Keep me going."

Not long ago, I partook in a Zoom meeting about a "moral

pub," an Irish bar in upper Manhattan called "Coogan's," which had just gone under. It had pulled its shutters down forever during the city's first COVID lockdown in March 2020. In this meeting, organized by Columbia University's Department of Medical Humanities and Ethics, I thought of Bloom and his moral pub and of how public characters bring a little dignity and warmth to an often cold and heartless city life. Coogan's was a special moral pub full of public characters. Though Irish, flying the shamrock of the Emerald Isle, the surrounding neighborhood is Dominican, with Puerto Ricans and African Americans. So alongside the Clancy Brothers, Coogan's knew how to salsa and play the blues; and because New York Presbyterian Hospital, a non-profit university medical center (and Coogan's landlord), was nearby, a fair share of Jewish doctors likewise frequented the pub. Off-duty cops, firefighters, and schoolteachers were also regulars, the sociable and the solitary, blowing off steam or quietly decompressing.

Coogan's was a patchwork quilt reflecting the patchwork quilt that is New York itself. Its policy of social intimacy was the exact opposite of social distancing. As co-owner Dave Hunt said, "You're going to have to work hard not to be welcome here." But for every small business in New York, returns constantly brush up against operating costs, rents and payroll, against utilities and supplies and insurance premiums. Unforeseen closures—through pandemic or otherwise—will likely tip businesses over the edge. Even a moratorium on the rent, the sweat equity and spirit of owners Peter Walsh, Hunt, and Tess McDade, and their forty-odd loyal staff and the thousands of regulars and supporters, all that couldn't save Coogan's from its monthly lease of kitchen equipment and insurance; even rent-free, costs ran to $20,000 a month. The greatest Main Street in the land, Broadway, between West 168th and 169th Streets, was about to lose a little of its heart.

When it opened in 1985, Washington Heights outside was falling apart. Coogan's helped piece it back together, fixing it up from the inside, offering a homey space for all-comers, erasing class, racial, and religious boundaries—this as a crack war raged on neighboring streets. "We landed in Washington Heights," Peter Walsh remembered, "at a time when it was probably one of the most dangerous neighborhoods in the country. We decided, what a great place to open a bar!" In 1992, after the police shot an innocent man and large-scale riots and looting ran rampant, Coogan's stayed open for twenty-four hours, hosting an emergency backroom meeting between the police and local Dominican politicians, brokering a truce to the disturbances and an eventual change in policing practices in Washington Heights.

Over the years, Coogan's transformative role and its footprint in the neighborhood went beyond the steak and burger staple casual dining, becoming a watering hole that hosted weekly comedy clubs and karaoke nights, birthdays and bar mitzvahs, an annual 5k charity run, set up by Walsh in 1990 when stepping out on the streets was menacing—with runners, musicians and cheerers eventually taking back those streets. "Let's run where they sell drugs," Walsh said. And in recent years, every February, a few blocks down the road, the Armory indoor track stages the Millrose Games. Swarms of star athletes and families descended on Coogan's afterward, cheering as the winners get introduced to Walsh. This says nothing about the high jinks of St. Paddy's Day, nor how Manhattan's Democratic Party often conducted full-disclosure job interviews in Coogan's front room and fund-raisers in the back. One time, Rudy Giuliani, then running for New York Mayor, visited Coogan's, claiming he was the only Republican ever to do so. "Nah," said Walsh, correcting him, "Gerry Adams was here last week."

In 2018, New York-Presbyterian Hospital tried to jack up

Coogan's rent by $40,000 a month. It looked like our moral pub had met an amoral end, ringing its last orders. The *New York Times* effectively ran an obituary penned by Pulitzer Prize-winning reporter and Coogan's regular, Jim Dwyer. (The *Los Angeles Times* said of Dwyer's great book: "*Subway Lives* may be hard-boiled, but it's best understood as an epic poem, and Dwyer himself comes across as a faintly Homeric figure, a late-twentieth-century urban bard who finds something heroic in (and under) the mean streets of Gotham.") Thankfully, Dwyer's closing time swansong proved premature. Or rather, it became a peaceful call-to-arms. Everybody and anyone who knew Coogan's was disgusted. The neighborhood rose up. In a wave of public support, spearheaded by Lin-Manuel Miranda, the Broadway star and creator of the musical *Hamilton*, himself a frequenter of Coogan's since boyhood, 15,000 people signed an online petition. Three days later, the landlord backed down, renegotiating a new lease that satisfied everyone involved. Coogan's had been spared. That was, until COVID.

Peter Walsh is very much a Joycean public character, even having a diploma in Irish Literature from Dublin's Trinity College, Sam Beckett's old alma mater. "We're the oral news," he said of Coogan's in our Zoom encounter, remembering his bar in the present tense. "Any small business," he reckoned, "is the first local news you hear, and it's more than just asking what the weather is. You feel the pulse of a neighborhood in individually owned stores rather than chains. . . . A chain could never do that. They take the money and fly." Walsh is a staunch supporter of independent small businesses across America. He's adamant that "the reinvention of the city has to take place, and it has to take place on Main Street, with not only racial integration but also economic integration." He spoke lovingly and poignantly about Coogan's. "We didn't have a religion," he said. "There were no tribes. You walked in and you became part of us. Our hug was a handshake. We didn't care where you came from." "Coogan's was a safety valve in the neighborhood," he said, "a place you came into and immediately felt safe. We planted seeds of decency."

For Walsh, Coogan's became its own country, a microcosm of what New York is and what America ought to be. "Part of Coogan's beauty was it was full of wonderful artists. Not just the ones who painted but people who lived their lives. They were always creating something. Dominicans were always creating wonderful things. Musically, they were creating something, in their literature, even in their language, the way they spoke. There was always something going on. And you had Harlem next door. There was a wide openness to the place."

"People need safe familiarity," Walsh said. "They're always getting things torn out of their lives. The city is always being torn down. It's a vicious process. And the people who tear things down have no idea about the patch of earth they're tearing down, about how life goes on there."

For my Zoom intervention, I said we might imagine Bloom strolling up Broadway, entering Coogan's, New York's own Davy Byrne's, and feeling welcome and *included*. One public character would then encounter another, a barkeep like Peter Walsh. Public characters mediate between the inner sanctums of the pub and the outer reality of the street. They float in and out of each and bring one into dialogue with the other. Maybe we can conceive, I said, how a diverse microworld like Coogan's is an open forum where dubious political ideas get shredded, where they are discussed and dissed by ordinary people, challenged and questioned. This was always the tradition of the pubs I knew, coming of age in Liverpool. In the pub, you found out everything that was going on in the neighborhood and around town. Often a lot of the banter would channel into a kind of collective lucidity—provided the company was diverse enough. One thing you always did, everybody did, was ridicule politicians, cast a skeptical eye over *all* parliamentary politics and *all* politicians. We'd have pilloried the hell out of Boris Johnson, laughed our heads off at his buffoonish ways. Given him a national platform? It's hard to imagine.

Being in a "public house," in short, helped keep reactionary ideology at bay, acting as a sort of political bulwark. Home alone, in relative isolation, in front of a TV or radio, imbibing commercial inanities and reactionary bile, much right-drifting ideology tends to stick inside people's heads. By contrast, getting out once in a while, in a moral pub or bar, you're forced, willy-nilly, to engage with others, to confront diversity, to hear diverse ideas. You're compelled to think about the world beyond yourself, to think publicly and parallactically. It's a great learning exercise, and losing a place like Coogan's is to lose a place of collective education, a part of our strategic defense system.

Here we might remember what Louis Althusser said about ideology: that it's a form of interpellation, taking place as a hailing from across the street: *"Hey, you there!"* Somehow, instinctively, we listen up; we accept it is us being called. Demagogic bluster interpellates masses of people because calls have what Althusser labeled "a recognition function." Messages hit a reality buzzer somewhere inside the audience. Private people are exposed to it, easy pickings. It doesn't take long before they convince themselves of the need to believe these messages, even if they're likely lies. It's on the level of *feeling* that ideology gets through, where it stokes up visceral emotions.

In this respect, *misrecognition* becomes a vital arm of political resistance, for *not getting taken in by ideology*. I often think of spaces like Coogan's, of moral pubs, as places where people escape such interpellation, where they refuse to be the objects of reactionary identification. It's a repositioning that involves a certain distancing from mass media, counteracting any emotional empathy that listeners develop with the messages broadcast. We might say it requires a Bloomian parallactic response, something coolly *thinking*, not a monocular or a hot-headed outburst. All that sounds like the citizen's old tin box clattering along the street or the din of a Trump rally. Remember, in *Ulysses*, the populace in the street was "shouting and laughing" at the citizen, not electing him to power.

AFTER COOGAN'S CLOSED, THE documentary filmmaker Glenn Osten Anderson made a touching one-hour remembrance of Coogan's, dedicated to Jim Dwyer, who passed away in 2020, age sixty-three, of lung cancer, the same year as his beloved bar. (Dwyer's obituary appeared in the *New York Times*, October 8, 2020.) Anderson's film, *Coogan's Way*, draws on evocative historical footage of Coogan's glory days, plotting its fraught beginnings in Washington Heights, concluding at the very end, with its poignant demise under COVID; how the bar came to be, the personalities behind it, how it operated, its way of doing things, all now not only immortalized cinematically but immortalized as a Broadway block as well, corner of West 169th Street, which bears the green street sign, COOGAN'S WAY.

At one point in Anderson's film, Peter Walsh, sensing the end is nigh, mentions having a wake for Coogan's, a great party "celebrating" its death, holding a vigil over its body, before it's finally put to rest; a party where whisky gets spilled over Tim Finnegan. In the Irish pub ballad, the eponymous bricklayer, drunk up a ladder, falls and is thought dead. At his wake, somebody splashes whisky—the "water of life" in Gaelic—on Tim's head, only to have him suddenly leap up, bawling, "D'ye think I'm dead?" The ballad's theme of death and resurrection appealed to Joyce's scatological imagination, framing *Finnegans Wake* around it; forever fascinated by the potencies of fermentation, Joyce has Earwicker transfigure and resurrect into Tim Finnegan. Was Walsh, another whisky-drinking publican, dreaming of a similar resurrection of Coogan's, dreaming big like Earwicker after his fall?

Earwicker isn't called that for nothing. His is an "eartalk"; he's an "earwitness" to things, a "paradigmatic ear." He has an ear out for "fermented language," for what's said and heard in a bar, for being a city builder, for ambitions as an urban planner, for resurrecting a city from the rot. But he knows it's a stuttering manifesto he's proclaiming, voiced from the bottom up, not top down. "This seat of our city," dreams Earwicker, "it is of all sides pleasant, comfortable and wholesome . . . doubling megalopolitan poleetness . . . End a muddy crushmess! Abbreciades anew York gustoms." Coogan's Way was full of megalopolitan poleetness and New York gustoms. It tippled and slurred and gave you an earful. It bloomed like Bloom, through humble democratic streets.

10

IN THE DARK DAYS WHEN Trump bleated and tweeted in the Oval Office, I visited Melbourne to participate in an "Ecocity

Summit." Climate change activist and Nobel Peace Laureate Al Gore starred, dishing the dirt about our inconvenient environmental truths, keynoting the jamboree gathering of global ecologists and environmentalists, greens and smart technologists, politicians and NGOs all intent on battling climate change in cities. We'd burned through a few fossil fuels ourselves, getting to Australia, but maybe something worthwhile could emerge from our collective emissions.

Al was slick and engaging, surprisingly self-deprecating. "You can imagine how I feel," he quipped, having a climate change denier heading the planet's biggest polluter. No names mentioned. The former U.S. vice president said he'd marched arm-in-arm with his daughter on the White House in a massive Peoples' Climate Day demo, never believing he'd ever see that day. Al's overall message was depressing; unprecedented droughts and wildfires, deforestation and downpours, hurricanes and tsunamis threaten the extinction of our species. One of his most unsettling images was footage from a helicopter ride he'd taken over Greenland, watching in real time its glaciers crumble into the sea.

The impact of sea level rises on the planet's urban populations, with their flimsily built, precariously positioned houses, is nigh catastrophic. They're tottering on the edge of oblivion. Nine thousand cities loom within sixty-two miles of the ocean. Cities with an elevation of less than three feet above sea level will go under unless protected. By the century's end, average sea levels are set to rise by these three feet. Even a rise of .4 inches puts one million people at risk. (I had to abandon Kim Stanley Robinson's novelistic projection of *New York 2140*, where sea levels had risen to the fourteenth floor of the old Met Life Building, because I found the thought of a Manhattan underwater too distressing. The poor paddled away in little dinghies while the rich whizzed by in speedboats and super-yachts, playing the stock market on water level fluctuations.)

Still, just as cities are threatened, they themselves threaten, collectively producing 70 percent of planetary greenhouse gas emissions. City economies squander resources, suck up water, sizzle holes in the ozone, create immense waste, and pollute their residents. And things could worsen: the International Energy Agency warns that business-as-usual practices in cities spell 50 percent emission hikes by 2050.

However, there's perhaps rosier news. For cities are launching their own fight back, the C40 alliance—a global network of ninety-one cities representing 650 million citizens, committed to delivering on the Paris Agreement. They're taking the lead as national governments balk. Thus, when Donald Trump refused to pledge $100 billion a year in climate finance, saying "I was elected to represent the citizens of Pittsburgh, not Paris," Pittsburgh's then-mayor, William Peduto, told his then-president otherwise.

In a *New York Times* op-ed (co-written with Paris's Mayor Anne Hidalgo, Chair of the C40 Alliance), Peduto reminded Trump how once-smokestack Pittsburgh is now a "trailblazer in environmental innovation," from wind turbines lighting up its bridges, investment in smart infrastructure, bike sharing programs and new mass transit, to a renewable energy industry that employs thirteen thousand people. And the city's Phipps Conservatory is widely recognized as one of the world's greenest buildings, generating its own energy and reusing all water. By 2035, Pittsburgh hopes to be 100 percent renewable-energy-powered, pledging, along with 250 other U.S. cities, "WE'RE STILL IN!" "and will achieve and exceed America's commitment to the Paris Agreement."

Cities as green leaders!

AND THEN CAME COVID. Ecologist Andreas Malm wonders why nation-states clamp down on COVID yet not on climate? More precisely, in *Corona-Climate-Chronic Emergency* (2020), he asks: "Why did they at best pay lip service to the ideal of doing something about emissions, and then shied away from any measures—not even putting their populations under house arrest—to repulse the coronavirus-associated disease formally designated COVID-19 by the WHO?"

One hypothesis is that COVID poses an immediate clinical threat, sudden scary death, whereas the environment is more distant, less immediately threatening. But Malm doesn't buy this line. "Global warming," he says, "will burn through the foundations of human life," eventually frazzling *everybody*. COVID is never likely to reach such mutually assured destruction, no matter how many it might kill. By doing nothing, climate pioneer Greta Thunberg says, you're leaving it to us kids to clean up adults' mess. But we're too young, and by the time we've grown up, it'll be too late. "I want you to act as you would in a crisis," Thunberg urges. "I want you to act as if your home is on fire. Because it is."

Malm cites one commentator saying, "the virus has just one cause," while climate change "is a highly complex issue." Again, Malm begs to differ: "if anything," he thinks, "the reverse seems truer." The climate movement, as well as intelligent science, have fingered a single source of blame: *fossil capital*. Indeed, scientific agencies now generally identify one solution: stop the emissions of greenhouse gases spewed out by the corporate sector. The UN's Intergovernmental Panel on Climate Change (IPCC) sets a timeline until 2040, aiming for temperatures to peak at a 1.6° C (34.8° F) rise. Yet achieving this target will require dramatic shifts in planetary business practices.

IPCC scientists drafted necessary criteria for fossil fuel energy reduction as an interim guideline, recommending no net additions to current coal or gas plants. They suggested a decrease in meat-based diets, altering urban space and built environments, "providing better human services with less expenditure of energy," and "new, more sustainable cities." Nonetheless, sound science here was categorically squashed. Big oil and vested private interests lobbied national politicians, who quickly capitulated, assuring a watering down of the document.

Australia objected to wording about reducing coal-fired plants; Saudi Arabia disliked "accelerated mitigation" phrasing; Argentina and Brazil's meat lobby had it in for references to meat reduction. The label "degrowth" equally had to be scrapped. In the end, the redacted report eradicated a clear scientific consensus; as John Bellamy Foster concluded in *Monthly Review* (June 2022), the document "should be entirely dismissed as the consensus of capital, and the betrayal of science, reason and humanity." That same month, the *Washington Post* (June 27, 2022) headlined: "World Pledged to Cut Methane. Emissions are Rising Instead." A few days later (June 30, 2022), the U.S. Supreme Court struck down the Environmental Protection Agency's plan to regulate and reduce carbon emissions from power plants, hobbling anybody's ability to fight climate change.

Andreas Malm says climate change and COVID revolve around the active production of *pandemicity*; not only from excessive use of pesticides and antibiotics cascading down the food chain, becoming breeding grounds for zoonotic disease and parasites to gnaw away at animals and our lungs; but also how capital itself is a "meta-virus," something that parasitizes our brains and bodies, fracks human as well as biophysical resources, plunders nature alongside human nature, creating a metabolic rift between each. It plagues cities, too, parasitizes

*livable for who*
*unaffordable*

them, and explains why many urban regions are so hazardous and so costly.

Cities are fair game to be fracked even more. After the promise of reductions in $CO_2$ emissions—glimpsed during lockdowns with less vehicular traffic and an exodus of a resource-squandering rich—cities seem ripe again for super-expropriation. The gains (and lessons) have been rolled back, tossed into the dustbin of history, lidded, already long forgotten. More disturbingly, $CO_2$ emissions have begun to exceed even pre-COVID rates. Meanwhile, parasites have profited enormously from the COVID pandemic, growing evermore massively wealthy. Now they're set to get richer still, making clean money from dirty capitalism.

AT THE ECOCITY SUMMIT, LOCAL boosters made a big deal about Melbourne's "world's most livable city" status, its sixth successive year of chart-topping success. After strolling along South Wharf's riverside promenade, amid smiling tourists gently toasted by glorious winter sunshine, I wasn't going to disagree. Although I recall back then also reading the roster of the world's least affordable cities, based on housing costs. Our most unaffordable city was Hong Kong; hot on its heels was Australia's very own Sydney; third came London, a city that had priced me out long ago; San Francisco ran fourth; and fifth, close behind, was the fair city of Melbourne.

Australia had two of the least affordable cities on earth, both eminently livable, each preeminently unaffordable. Thus the low-tech question: most livable for whom? What does livability mean in the context of sustainability? How resilient can a city be when access is denied to all but its wealthiest people? When citizens of Sydney grumbled that their city was getting just too expensive, Australia's then-Deputy Prime Minister, Barnaby

Joyce, had these words of anti-sympathy: "Get out!" Joyce was fed up with people griping about the unaffordability of Sydney and Melbourne. If you can't stand the heat, get out of the kitchen. (Funnily enough, I'd heard a similar refrain from ex-New York City mayor Michael Bloomberg, a purported great patron of public health and environmental concerns.) Maybe Barnaby Joyce, like Michael Bloomberg, is unaware that, as temperatures heat up, not everybody has A/C.

Climate action plans get imaginatively formulated by scientists and social movements, yet national politicians lack the guts to confront a polluting private sector, deflecting the affordable housing and fossil capital question. On the other hand, they're more than happy to endorse a boom in for-profit renewable energies and the recruitment of management consultancies as they downsize public budgets, purging municipal coffers in their relentless pursuit to privatize vital social infrastructure.

On this note, it's interesting to compare the latest hit list of "the most livable cities," compiled for 2022 by *The Economist*'s Intelligence Unit (EIU). One hundred and seventy-three cities around the world were ranked on a "Global Livability Index," totted up from various factors—healthcare, crime rates, political stability, infrastructure, access to green space. This is the first real post-COVID league table, and the formula of what now constitutes "livable" has altered somewhat.

London, Paris, and New York are nowhere: too costly, too unstable (Brexit London), and too divided. The "winners" tend to herald from smaller, soberer, European cities. Vienna leads the way, Copenhagen second, then Zurich. Canadian cities fared well: Calgary fourth, Vancouver fifth, and Toronto eighth, all with strong public health systems. Geneva sixth, Frankfurt seventh, Amsterdam ninth, and Melbourne and Osaka tied for tenth.

The EIU report said top cities have "stability, good infrastructure and services, as well as enjoyable leisure activities." Australian cities lost out because of higher COVID infection rates, stricter border controls, and slow vaccination rollouts. Conversely, European and Canadian cities benefited from faster vaccination uptakes, enabling lockdown restrictions to ease earlier. Although the question of affordability looms forever large, COVID has at least rocked a little sense into people, a recognition that public resources are valuable for livability.

So, too, is democracy. The year I visited Melbourne's Ecocity Summit was timely because it coincided with the Golden Jubilee of Henri Lefebvre's *The Right to the City*, the French philosopher's other great urban book, his inaugural "cry and demand" for more participatory urban life. The right to the city might seem like a fuzzy sort of human right. But really, it is very concrete. It means the right to live out the city as one's own, to be happy there, to have affordable housing, decent schools for your kids, accessible services (like free healthcare), reliable public transport, clean air and water. It's the right to have your urban horizon as wide or as narrow as you want, to feel some sense of shared purpose, that you're not alienated from the city's affairs. If you have this right, there's a greater likelihood that you'll respect your duty toward the city and appreciate your obligation to the greater common good. You might better understand that the city itself is a great public work and that you are part of it.

Under our current phase of capitalism, though, cities have become vortexes for sucking in everything the planet offers— capital and power, culture and people, wealth and dispensable labor power—and spitting out what it doesn't need. It's this sucking in and spitting out of people and goods, of capital and information, that fuels the urban machine, that makes cities so dynamic as well as so destabilizing, so profitable yet so socially and environmentally toxic. Cities expel "surplus" people just as labor markets expel superfluous workers, spewing them out, secreting what Lefebvre calls a *residue*. It's an expulsion process that expands urban space, has it push itself out, spreads its remit, entangles rural space, disentangles rural life.

Who are residues? They're workers without regularity, salaries, and security, workers without any real stake in the future of work. They're refugees rejected and rebuked, profiled and patrolled no matter where they wander, victims of war and economic collapse, environmental devastation, drought and deforestation, wildfires and wild regimes. They're displacees, too, people forced off the land, thrown out of housing, dispossessees. Residues aren't merely the city's secretion: they're now the very substance of the city itself. Lefebvre says the political ante is to formulate a "revolutionary conception of citizenship." Indeed, he said this is really what he meant by the right to the city all along.

ONE OF THE HIGHLIGHTS OF my visit to Melbourne was a stunning exhibition called "EXIT" at the Ian Potter Museum of Art. EXIT was the brainchild of the late Paul Virilio (1932-2018), an urbanist clearly marked by Lefebvre's work on space and everyday life because EXIT offered graphic insight into our planet of residues and refugees. A life-size Virilio greeted you upon entering the museum, actually a three-and-a-half-minute video of the philosopher heading toward the camera (and toward you), marching along the Atlantic seafront at La Rochelle in western France, where Virilio used to live. "The twenty-first century will be the century of great migration," Virilio said. Over the next fifty years, a billion people will be displaced because of climatic catastrophe, war, and economic breakdown, a never-ending procession of human movement, an EXIT of unprecedented magnitude.

In the main EXIT installation, everything went dark. You sat on the floor, and before you, a giant globe moved, planet earth revolving and orbiting in bright fluorescent color, shifting back and forth. You were immersed in it. You heard its whooshing motion, listened to liquid gurgling, to sea levels rising. Red and green pixels mapped out the inexorable flow of refugees and displacees, a global visual torrent: between January 2000 and April 2015, 186,280,653 people have been disrupted because of drought; 745,277,081 by storms; 27,586,735 by earthquakes. "Natural" disasters displace, on average, twenty-six million people annually—one person every second. Between January 2006 and December 2014, 124 million people were displaced because of inundations, and we're still counting, likely exponentially, totting up hundreds of thousands more from recent Pakistan. Numbers, of course, are significantly higher in the Global South than in the Global North: countries most affected by global warming, we know, are least responsible for greenhouse gas emissions.

Over the next half-century, a tsunami of a billion displaced souls will form a vast human tidal wave, searching for a homeland, for a city, for a roof over their heads; a massive exodus of uprooted residues that will disrupt the geopolitics of nation-states and cities, a colossal flow that can't be dammed, that will need to be absorbed somewhere, somehow. No international law can protect these deportees. Many will end up in internment camps, confined on the edge of some big city, where they'll await reintegration or further expulsion. A lot will never leave. People are on the move, yet national frontiers close down; walls go up (or try to), even in non-pandemic times.

EXIT was the development of an earlier Virilio project called *Terre Natale: Stop Eject*, realized in collaboration with the French photographer and filmmaker Raymond Depardon. The Ian

Potter Museum bookstore had this exhibition's handsome cata-
log, a large-formatted brick of a book full of Depardon's evocative, globetrotting images, many in color; he's been to the four
corners of the world, scouring our lonely planet for disappearing cultures and ecologically devastated landscapes. Depardon
is fascinated by indigenous cultures and languages threatened
with extinction, with peoples on the margins of globalization, like
Brazil's Northeastern Yanomanis.

Virilio, a Parisian, didn't much like traveling; Depardon, of
peasant stock, whose parents hardly left their village, journeys
everywhere. Their exposition is a confrontation between the
countryside and the city, between the rooted and the uprooted,
between the poetics of attachment and detachment. But there's a
twist to this opposition, Virilio says, because it "not only calls into
question the countryside and rural roots, but urban roots as well."
"We're seeing the end of the city and therefore the end of urban
exile." We're heading toward "THE BEYOND CITY," Virilio
says, "not a city of belonging but a city of movement." Migratory
movement involves a constant "stopping and ejecting." You stop,
and you eject the cassette. "We've gone from a place of election—
where we elect to live and vote—to a place of ejection and disen-
franchisement. Stop eject means, *'Get Out of Here!'*"

Virilio, like Lefebvre, wonders what this might spell for solidarity. Indeed, what might a new revolutionary conception of
citizenship actually entail? Is it a citizenship that lies inside and
beyond a passport and any official documentation? Struggled
for, not rubber-stamped? A citizenship without a flag, without
a country, without borders? An urban citizenship? One strand
of this, presumably a kind of indemnity insurance that future-
proofs our endangered ecology, would be a new hospitality for
cities, a right to the city that leaps across the nationalist divide,
that sneaks inside it, under its reactionary radar.

Within this right, "cities of refuge" might be created: the right to the city would thus be the right to an urban immunity, an urban asylum for the rootless and landless, an unconditional citizenship attached to a city; an urban re-enfranchisement beyond any ecology conceived by mayors and political honchos, drawing its energy from below, safeguarding the downtrodden and disaffected, offering sanctuary for every residual, for every stranger and settler among us.

The ideal mightn't be as far-fetched as it sounds. We'd heard the likes in the Bible, from Numbers 35:11–28, and we've heard it not long ago voiced in several U.S. cities—Austin, Boston, Chicago, Los Angeles, New York, Oakland, Philadelphia, Providence, and San Francisco—that refused to cooperate with Trump's promise to deport millions of undocumented immigrants. Across the United States, "sanctuary cities" had opposed the federal government and its immigration agents; prodded by immigrant rights and citizens' groups, these urban bastions affirmed their intention to defy the national administration, risking losing millions of dollars in federal support as they pledged to act as bulwarks against mass deportation. Cities, as yet, have no power to bestow "official" rights to people. But they have the power to resist and can resist in our age of pandemic and climatic crisis. In the face of national political illegitimacy, the specter of urban solidarity haunts. Let it haunt.

This is only one piece of the necessary contract. Another aspect of ecological sustainability is a new right *of* the city, a new status for the city itself, thereby releasing what I'd like to call *double indemnity urbanism*: a right *to* and *of* the city. Double indemnity insurance is life assurance that makes a double payment to the beneficiary upon accidental death. Here the policy would have a similar dual aspect—paying out twice—yet hopefully avoiding accidental death, even premeditated death, the premeditated death of a city. Double indemnity insurance policies usually cover people working in "hazardous industries;" engaging in progressive urban politics is an equally risky business these days. Double indemnity sees the city through twin lenses, has binocular vision, is a Bloomian parallax that conjoins urban and environmental politics.

The C40 alliance has let us glimpse the promise of this parallax. Cities are more progressive than nation-states. We knew it and continue to see it all around us. U.S. cities initiate minimum wage ordinances, instigate paid sick days, draft lesbian, gay, bisexual, and transgender rights—only to have their conservative states block this legislation. Michigan cities once proposed a bill to restrict plastic bags, cups and packaging in restaurants and fast-food outlets, non-biodegradable sources of pollution. Yet the state's Restaurant Association, after aggressive and successful lobbying, prevented chain restaurants and retailers from complying. Texas's big cities propose a ban on fracking, but the state, responding to big gas and oil lobbies, caves in, duly bans the ban. Rancorous stand-offs between state and city, national government and municipalities punctuate the United States' political landscape; they'll doubtless continue to intensify in a post-Roe world. "We're the United States of America," conservative state representatives remind people, implying that they're not the "United Cities of America."

Even so, the concept of "united cities" is a thrilling one, not only in America; an urban alliance that stretches across the globe, something that ramps up the political stakes much more radically than the C40 network, bestowing greater democratic and ecological powers on cities—powers to act and self-govern, to do so alongside other cities, a collectivity of democratic units, of unit structures. That said, it's difficult to reimagine cities with more jurisdictional powers, with new empowering rights, if they're not inclusive, if their resources aren't accessible to everyone and all but the privileged are kept out—like in "compact city" ideals, which create zones of clean, gated exclusivity, ripe for techno-fixes and monopoly exploitation, for topping livability indices. Urban dwellers must lobby their city mayors to lobby their state and federal governments, scaling up climate concerns, engaging in mass education programs in communities about the realities of climate change. If not, urban citizens need to oust mayors, vote them out or throw them out of office, together with any regional and national leaders denying the urgency of climate mitigation.

Parallax, meanwhile, has another strand to seeing double: bringing the participation-representation dialectic to bear on each other, to have one empower the other, to reinforce one another. It's to see how pressure from below—from urban communities and social movements, from responsible, engaged citizens—might reshape what happens above; that participation can affect representation; that resistance from the outside might hook up with the inside, transform the inside. It might give members of the inside the incentive, as well as the courage, to step out of the closet, to embrace their constituents. "Official" representatives in government and municipalities, those in public office, might be kept on their toes by a citizens' movement exerting pressure from this outside, in public squares and in alternative media, pamphleting and petitioning, demonstrating in the street, maybe even in the labs, where sound science might become a responsible arm of the people, something honestly in the public interest.

Participation implies rights, representation suggests duties. But in "speaking for" participants, representatives need to listen to them and encourage participation. Together, in dialogue, representatives and participants can formulate a new mandate for the greater collective good, a new program *for* the city, a new right *of* the city, of *their* city. Guy Debord used to say everything that was

directly lived has moved away into a representation. He meant
it has moved into a representation done from above, a representation of money power, of career politicians, a representation of
banks and Wall Street, of management consultancy "experts,"
a representation of their spectacular, seductive images and lies.
Representative "democracy" has wrenched itself away from participatory democracy is what he meant, from the lived reality of
participants; we need to stitch it back again, unite the lived with
the represented, participation with representation, forge a closer
common understanding of each, have representation represent
the lived.

Maybe then we might see ordinary progressive people
develop enough collective muscle to participate alongside official
representatives. One is compelled to answer to the other, doing
so in public service delivery, in the creation of a more socially
just urban policy. It's surely not hard to imagine how, in times
of crisis, at moments when there's urgent need for collective
necessity—like during COVID—that saner and more thoughtful
political responses might be worked out. They might be worked
out and worked through with other cities. Instead of opaque,
behind-the-scenes machinations, secret wheeling and dealings
convened by fudging and fumbling politicians, we might witness transparency and real communication, real public engagement—real democratic assembly in decision making, an antidote
to privatized disassembly. We might see a kind of double-action
democracy unfold, the outside helping democratize the inside.

Seeing cities at the forefront of life and politics makes a lot
of sense. Urbanization continues apace; people increasingly lead
urban lives. It's not that everybody inhabits cities so much as
even as people leave, flee cities, we're all nonetheless touched by
the culture of urbanism, ever more touched by it, by its economics and politics, by its immense social sway: we all live out urban

existences whether we think it or not, whether we like it or not, whether we still work in the city, or whether we work at home away from the city. Whatever: we're still likely working *for* the city, tapping an urban market somehow (crucial for agriculture production), working for an organization with a city base, with an urban orbit, with an urban power. Urbanism is global—planetary, if we can accept Lefebvre's stellar terminology; it's an intricate and inextricable "way of life" for everybody.

Urban boundaries have become more porous and intermingled, more hybrid and messy; yet nation-states try to dam the flow, erect barriers and repress diversity—barriers, that is, for people: political leaders gleefully cheer on capital circulating without apparent limit or hindrance. A new progressive status for cities has to be something else; it has to manage and administer differently. The mosaic and mentality need rebooting. This new status would involve both a shrinking and enlargement of the scale of governance, below the nation-state yet wider than city government.

It would mean a regional scale of metropolitan control, a "city-state" configuration, like in Ancient Greece, where there were no nation-states as such; identity took on an urban characterization, got defined by which city you belonged to, and belonging was always portable and transferable. This new city-state could be mobilized so that its reactionary hinterlands would get neutralized, incorporated within the city-state's domain; a form of progressive gerrymandering, you might wonder? Yes. God knows it's about time political redistricting promoted common betterment rather than exclusive plundering.

Maybe we could celebrate its inauguration with a "Funeral Oration" for the COVID dead, along the lines of Pericles's famous oration commemorating the city's Peloponnesian War dead. Pericles (495–429 BC) is the sort of urban leader we need more than ever, a man with parallax vision who straddled the representative-participatory divide. Flawed, needless to say, yet he was a *populist* before the label received a bad rap, before it became ideological and reactionary. His "Funeral Oration," narrated by Thucydides in *The Peloponnesian War*, delivered in 431 BC before plague (typhoid fever) eventually saw him off, remains the greatest ever paean to Athens's democratic *openness*, to its lack of walls, to its inclusive public spaces; a civic pride that stands as the nemesis to Sparta's militarism—and to bellicose nationalism everywhere.

"We throw open our city to the world," said Pericles, "and never by alien acts exclude foreigners from any opportunity of learning or observing, although the eyes of an enemy may occasionally profit by our liberality; trusting less in the system and policy than to the native spirit of our citizens." Pericles believed that Athens's liberality never hindered its greatness: "Advancement in public life falls to reputations for capacity, class considerations not being allowed to interfere with merit . . . our ordinary citizens, though occupied with the pursuits of industry, are still fair judges of public matters . . . at Athens we live exactly as we please, and yet are just as ready to encounter every legitimate danger."

It's a beautiful imaginary of how we might rezone our plague-infested Zone, the Zone that Thomas Pynchon set out for us at the beginning of this book. The great twentieth-century urban historian Lewis Mumford was someone who loved such a Hellenic vision of urban democracy and eulogized it in his own monumental oration, *The City in History* (1961), which he concluded with a birth, not a death. To be sure, Mumford gave us a startlingly suggestive expression of what this city-state might look like in our own times, how it might function. There'd no longer be any metropolitan region dominated by a single center, he says, positioned within its endlessly sprawling structure.

What we'd have instead is a regional framework "capable of embracing cities of many sizes, including the metropolitan center," an "open-ended network" comparable to "an electric power grid." "Each unit of the system has a certain degree of self-sufficiency and self-direction. . . . But by being linked together, the power stations form a whole system whose parts, though relatively independent, can upon demand work as a whole, and make good what is lacking in any particular area." Those power stations, need we add, would be non-coal-fired.

The old function of the urban center, as a walled container, would be exercised through the functional grid, a framework Mumford intriguingly calls "the invisible city." We're seemingly back full circle to Marco Polo and Kublai Khan, to dreams trying to correspond with reality. In the meantime, the "visible city" would constitute something like our old configuration, still existent, perhaps even more apparent, where forms and functions are more concrete. The visible city would be the city of face-to-face encounters and meetings, of place-specific everyday life, with explicitly defined neighborhoods.

But the invisible city, as a parallel universe—a parallax universe, we might say—would flow through the visible city. Relations are more abstract, more virtual, operating, as Mumford says, through a process of "etherealization." "Gone is primitive local monopoly through isolation; gone is the metropolitan monopoly through seizure and exploitation. The ideal mission of the city is to further this process of cultural circulation and diffusion; and this would restore to many now subordinate urban centers a variety of activities that were once drained away for the exclusive benefit of the great city."

Mumford says a "new urban constellation" would prevail, which today we might see as a resilient and sustainable urban form, "capable of preserving the advantage of smaller units, yet enjoying the scope of large-scale metropolitan organization," encouraging more diverse forms of urban agriculture and neutralizing exploitative urban and rural divisions of labor. Maybe we might see it reversing the metabolic rift that has torn apart our relations with nature, that's opened up a chasm about to swallow us up. Importantly, mutual intercourse would base itself on cooperation, "passing through geographic obstacles and national barriers as readily as X-rays pass through solid objects." Over time, this system "could embrace the whole planet."

The technological prowess to realize this parallax city, this city of visibility and invisibility, is here, now, already within our grasp; I'd glimpsed it at the base of the Ecocity Summit. At its apex, it lurks in bourgeois commercial clothing. If only we could shrug this off, break free, ditch the suits and ties, the business cards and profit motives, if only we could find the political will to liberate our cities and ourselves. Media and technology have undergone extraordinary innovation and experimentation over recent decades, making them super-dynamic sectors of our lives. Yet politics has stagnated; our political institutions haven't changed for centuries. (British Parliament still has its politicians sit on the same medieval benches Guy Fawkes tried to blow up!) In politics, there's been no reimagining, no experimentation, no innovation.

Perhaps this is intentionally so, done for solid reasons of preservation, of defending vested interests. If voting really changed anything, they'd abolish it anyway. What changes there have been always seem to prop up the status quo rather than overturn it—or if they do overturn it, it moves in an even more retrogressive direction, like the United States' current Supreme Court. Our political institutions have imbricated themselves, implicated themselves, plonked themselves down on us at an ever more rigid national scale. This has to change, be challenged, fought over, and struggled to be changed. We need to buy into another politics with another policy, a double insurance package, a right *to* and *of* the city, here and there. This is the future. It can no longer be elsewhere nor later.

## 11

SINCE BEGINNING THIS BOOK, the COVID crisis has undergone assorted mutations and phases, mutations in virus strains, phases in its handling and social adaptation—from acute crises of lockdowns and quarantines, mass deaths and hospitalizations, to vaccine rollouts and the latest easing of social distancing and face-mask mandates. Each of the preceding chapters largely reflects these phases, has journeyed through them, been written around them. They've tried to periodize urban life and COVID over the past two years, tried to locate the troubled state of this author's mind as well as the troubled state of our world.

In everyday life, there's general acceptance that COVID is probably here to stay, like severe flu strains, and that life must go on, even if working life might never be quite what it was. Infections remain high. They may get higher still. Yet hospitalizations and death rates dip. And although it's unclear what lies ahead, what other variants might plague us in the future—whether the next Big One will strike—relative "normality" seems to have returned to most cities. New York's subway and London's underground are almost as busy as ever; ditto Paris's Métro; crowds in both Soho and SoHo are as dense and as intense as before, busy to the point of jostling one another for step-space on the sidewalk. One spring Saturday afternoon jaunt along Prince Street was the busiest I'd ever seen. It could be, then, that, no matter what, many people never stop yearning for the thrills of the big city. The thirst to gulp its experience down is unquenchable.

But there are darker recesses to the human psyche, other plagues that appear never to want to go away, forever contaminating people's lives. Alas, we've no vaccine for them yet. War, genocide, mass shootings—a whole gamut of destruction and devastation, diabolical given they've followed a pandemic that has already slaughtered millions. The Russian invasion of Ukraine has knocked our global food and fuel supplies into a tailspin, highlighting the fragility of both under a paradigm of ever more corporate domination and monopoly.

Efficiency drives and competitive advantage threaten our food systems just as they threaten our cities and climate. Ukraine supplies 36 percent of the world's sunflower oil. Both Ukraine and Russia are massive suppliers of the world's wheat. War means these staples will become scarcer and more expensive. The world faces the greatest cost of living crisis in a generation. Food prices are at near record highs. Inflation is rising rapidly everywhere. Rents and housing costs soar. Wages stagnate. Economy, energy, climate, conflict, and COVID all now collide and conspire to exacerbate existing vulnerability and inequity.

If life isn't quite nasty, brutish, and short, then people are certainly angry, anxious, and hungry. A general malaise prevails. You can feel it wafting. You don't need a weatherman to know which way the wind blows. There are scant reasons to be cheerful right now. And in the United States, the overruling of Roe v. Wade by the Supreme Court, rescinding abortion rights in many states, coupled with its voting down of bolder environmental protection, sends retrogressive messages rippling throughout the planetary airwaves.

But despite everything, or maybe because of everything, even in the rubble of what's left of Ukrainian cities, life goes on, has to go on. There is little choice for ordinary people but to carry on or try to. We can't go on, the *dramatis personae* of Beckett were fond of saying: *They go on*. "You must go on," says Beckett's unname-able, like so many unnameables in so many unnameable places, "you must say words, as long as there are any."

Maybe to go on, to keep on keeping on, unnameables need to continue to say words and uphold another kind of parallactic vision. They need to see that the global and the local, the big, long wave, essentially abstract forces that condition our lives—that frequently depress our lives—and the reality of this life itself, our everyday life, are united yet separate. Ironically, perhaps it's no bad thing to see both realms as separate. Maybe this is the best dialectical manipulation we can deploy to maintain Gramsci's pessimism of the intellect and optimism of the will. To feel the immediate weight of the world on one's shoulders, to hear the bad news daily in the news, is often too much, too paralyzing to permit meaningful action and activism. Up against those odds, everything you do seems not enough, too trivial.

But if you can push aside the big bad news and get on practi-cally with smaller, potentially good news, life seems more bear-able and changeable. It means you can press on and do what you can wherever you are, wherever you find yourself, in what-ever locality and neighborhood. There, you can derive suste-nance and find camaraderie with others. You can empower one another, engage yourselves, and see where it might lead. Your agenda might be a sort of shopping list attached to the fridge by a magnet, an ABCD of what you might do today, now, with others. (Remember, ABCD stands for "Asset-Based Community Development.") This modus operandi is one way of not letting the world get ahead of itself, of *not* bringing it all back home. The world's problems are just too vast to pass through your doorway. Instead, you begin with things that might be achievable in the meanwhile, and even that is likely to be hard.

Is this a reversal of the belief that long-wave history is on our

side, that past experience suggests our future will improve? It
could be. There's no guarantee that improvement is the case.
Maybe the only future, especially the only environmental future,
is shorter range, what you do *now*, what common ground you
find with other unnameables. Out of this common ground, some
wider terrain of engagement might open up, helping change the
course of tomorrow and, in its cumulative effect, change the day
after tomorrow, too, thus changing a longer-range future. It's a
little piece of a bigger jigsaw puzzle. But to complete the game,
you painstakingly have to focus on finding each little slot, each
piece that fits, and the pieces that fit around that piece. So that
after a while, the totality of all the little pieces adds up, collectively composing the patterning of the entire structure.

This amounts to putting bigger social reality in its context,
finding its constitutive little pieces, being able to play each piece
each day, playing the game as Henri Lefebvre played the game of
*everyday life*: "as the inevitable starting point for the realization
of the possible." Each trivial bit has significance, each daily life.
This is Joyce's point in *Ulysses*: how a boring day in early twentieth-century Dublin, of no importance whatsoever, is endowed
with epic consequence. Joyce has Stephen Dedalus announce
that history isn't something made from above—isn't the mani-
festation of God or "officially" made by God-like heroes—but "*a
shout in the street*." All we can do is bawl out ourselves in streets
we know, do so in our own quiet or loud manner, slotting in one
piece of the puzzle at a time.

SOMEONE INTO PUZZLES WAS the French writer Georges
Perec (1936–1982), who wrote a novel about pieces of the city,
about the home, actually a series of homes in a single apartment
building, creating a macrocosm of Paris from an apparently

insignificant microcosm. The book bore a revealing title, revealing because of the significance it confers on something small: *Life: A User's Manual*. This might have been only one piece of an immense urban puzzle—the city of Paris itself—but without it and its other pieces, there would be no complete image, no substance to the whole puzzle. The puzzle is readable only when it is assembled. But without its pieces, there's nothing to assemble. "Yes," writes Perec, "it could begin this way, right here, just like that, in a rather slow and ponderous way...where people pass by almost without seeing each other, where the life of the building regularly and distantly resounds."

Perec was obsessed with the idea of visualizing an apartment building as if the entire façade had been removed, exposing every room on every floor, every detail of the lives led within. When I was reading his rendering of this idea, the ingenious *Life* novel, which delves into each room at 11, rue Simon-Crubellier (a fictitious address), going deeper and deeper into the habitants within, forming a compendium of interrelated stories, at once humorous, bizarre, and realistic, I happened upon an article in the *New York Times* ("A Landlord 'Underestimated' His Tenants," May 6, 2022) about a single building in the South Bronx, at 700 East 134th Street. Its motley crew of residents wasn't too unreminiscent of those of Perec's apartment. Poorer doubtless, but as patchwork a cloth as you'd find anywhere in the world, a heterogeneous assortment of tenants.

The Bronx building, the article said, was bought by a landlord for $4 million. He immediately threatened to raise the rents and kick the tenants out. South Bronx neighborhoods have become a popular stomping ground for rich developers with big plans for upscaling poor parts of the city, for plucking up properties for a relative song. Yet on East 134th Street, tenants banded together, navigated a complicated New York City legal case, and managed to stave off harassment and multiple attempts by the landlord to evict them. A few of these tenants had been homeless; others were unemployed. Some had jobs—one was a chef, another a photographer; others a nurse, metal worker, substitute teacher, and digital printer, all earning modest incomes. It was an oddball mix, which would have delighted Perec's offbeat brain, kindled his creative imagination.

As it happened, these tenants had plenty of imagination themselves and found that they could communicate with one another and that they shared a common cause: the struggle against high rents. That they were motley and diverse also meant they had a diverse array of skills, latent skills that some never recognized or realized could be pooled together. Rather than create disunity, they provided the ingredients for an unusual campaign of unity. One tenant discovered she was a good writer; another, jobless, had time to visit city government offices and gather information, to hit the legal books and learn about tenant rights; the photographer took pictures, documenting the deliberate disrepair of the building. Another tenant had a friend in state housing who could make calls. And so on. . . .

An older tenant suspected that the building might legally be rent-stabilized. Thus, even if the existing tenants were removed, the landlord would still face that barrier in the future. This became a key point of leverage. After inspecting historical records, tenants found that the building was indeed rent-stabilized; and when the tenants were introduced to the non-profit Urban Homesteading Association Board, they not only received legal advice; the board also found a novel way to refinance the building and turn it over to the tenants to run as a co-op. It was a miraculous game-changer, an incredible change of fortunes.

Recognizing he was on a losing ticket, the landlord was bought out, and the building was then handed over to the tenants who, as

de facto original shareholders, had the option to buy their apartments at a discounted $2,500 apiece! In the end, a single building in the South Bronx, a little bit of New York's bigger puzzle, became a potential board game that other tenants and activists in the city could "play," that they could similarly piece together. It required unity and application, courage to engage in a losing battle and somehow overcome, to do it at home. "Join the Fight for Housing Rights," one of the new co-owner's T-shirt read. "We will win," he said, smiling. "Because we already won."

ONE OF THE PRINCIPAL COMPONENTS in this fight was *remembering*, remembering the everyday past, a past that landlords and developers, intent on exploiting their properties, often try to deny or wipe out, make people forget (like a rent-stabilized past). It's amazing how quickly you forget, isn't it, how, upon seeing an empty lot in a familiar city, or a vacant unit along a familiar street, just what that lot or store was before getting demolished or shuttered up. And those former tenants and storekeepers, who were they, and where did they go?

Over the last decade of his life, Perec worked on an ambitious and strange project of remembering, remembering Paris's old urban environment. It was an intended book, never completed, that he was calling *Lieux* (*Places*). Yet people who knew Perec didn't forget, and this past spring (May 2022), just as the *New York Times*'s Bronx building article went to press, Perec's unfinished *Lieux* was reassembled and published in handsome book form by Éditions du Seuil. "I didn't want to forget," Perec said. "This is the core of the book."

"I have chosen twelve sites in Paris," he explained, "streets, squares, crossroads, linked by memories, to events or important moments of my existence." Each month, Perec said, "I'll describe two of these sites: once, on the spot (in a café, in the street), noting 'what I see' in a manner the most neutral possible. I'll enumerate the shops, details about the architecture, minor events (a fire-truck that passes, a woman who attaches her dog before entering a *charcuterie*, a removal van, posters on the wall, people coming and going); a second time, no matter where (at home, in a café or office), I'll describe these same places from memory, evoking the people linked to them, all the persons I can remember." At the end of one year, each of these sites—these *lieux*—will have been described twice, once from memory, the other time observed matter-of-factly, without emotional coloring.

Then, said Perec, he would do something special: he would put the entirety of the loose notes and jottings, all the bits of scrap paper he'd written on, all the photographs taken of these places, all the memorabilia he'd collected (Métro tickets, cinema tickets, bar slips, stubs, handouts, street maps), all the evidence of actually being there then—he'd put everything into separate envelopes marked by location and seal them with wax. His intention was that they'd represent *bombes du temps* (time-capsules), and at the end of twelve years—a timeline he'd never live to see—after every place had been described twice twelve times over, the envelopes would be opened. "I shall then know whether it was worth the effort. What I hope for from it," he said, "is nothing other than the record of a threefold experience of aging: of the places themselves, of my memories, and of my writing."

*Lieux*, the book, is a beautiful specimen capturing the wonderful idiosyncratic nature of Perec's "deciphering of pieces of the city." The notes on each site, the photos and contact prints, his doodles and maps, even a diagram of Perec's method of "constructing sets of mutually orthogonal Latin squares" (a system aided by an Indian mathematician at the University of North Carolina)—everything that was contained in those 288 wax-sealed envelopes has now been opened and reproduced in its original glory. It's a special document of a writer's life and of the life of Paris between the late 1960s and early 1980s, a moment when large-scale urban renewal and slum clearance, especially in eastern Paris, was tearing down and demolishing many of its old streets, slums or not.

One of Perec's major points of interest in *Lieux* is rue Vilin, in Belleville, in Paris's 20th arrondissement, where he passed his early childhood. Perec presents rue Vilin in loving detail, house by house, street number by street number—the restaurants and bistros, the cafés and hotels, the hairdressers and cobblers, the creameries and plumbers, the wine stores and coal merchants, the street urchins and women peeking out of darkened windows, the architecture and topography. Robert Doisneau took extensive photos of rue Vilin. Its staircase, which opened out onto one of the best panoramas of Paris, was said to be the loveliest in the whole of France, if not the world, featured in countless films, including Perec's own cinematic venture, from 1974 (co-directed with Bernard Queysanne), *Un Homme qui Dort*. Based around Perec's 1967 novel, the man who sleeps is the author's twenty-five-year-old alter ego, a student indifferent to the world, who not only sleeps a lot and sits introspectively in his garret (the film begins with him reading Henri Lefebvre's *Everyday life in the Modern World*), he's also out nocturnally pacing many of the locations of *Lieux*.

Number 24 rue Vilin was chez Perec, boarded up and ruined when we see it in the 1970s. All that existed, if the passerby stopped to look closely then, if they lingered awhile, was a very faded sign above a rotten doorframe: *COIFFURE DAMES*, the hairdresser's store once run by Perec's mother. The act of remembering, this image of Perec's past, becomes more poignant when we hear that she would perish at Auschwitz in 1943.

*Vilin*

IV

*Parc de Belleville*

*Métro Couronnes*

(Perec's father had died three years earlier from shrapnel wounds after enlisting in the French army, leaving Perec to be raised by his paternal aunt and uncle.)

Number 24 is hauntingly brought back to life by Robert Bober's magnificent homage to rue Vilin and to Perec, *En Remontant la rue Vilin*—going up rue Vilin again. The forty-eight-minute documentary, from 1992, is especially haunting because, in the 1980s, not long after Perec's death, rue Vilin had almost entirely disappeared, staircase and all, number 24 and all, wiped out and incorporated into an eleven-acre green space, Parc de Belleville, completed in 1988. If you didn't know it, hadn't seen the photos, read Perec's notes, seen Bober's film, you'd never believe this street from Perec's past had ever existed.

We might point the finger at Jacques Chirac. In 1977, he became Paris's mayor, the city's first-ever twentieth-century leader. Incredibly, between 1794 and 1977, Paris was the only city or town in the whole of France without a mayor. Yet once in office, Chirac rapidly made up for lost time. With new, unprecedented decision-making powers, he soon earned himself the epithet "the bulldozer," implementing widescale urban renewal, spearheaded by the *Plan Programme de L'Est de Paris* (1983). The scheme would gouge 4,000 acres out of the city's eastern working-class sector, disrupting a million-odd poorer residents, replacing the old urban fabric with new *espaces verts*, new green spaces, like Parc de Belleville, along with blocks of soulless housing projects. Much of Belleville was deemed beyond salvation, fit for the wreckers' ball, and swiftly demolished. Eric Hazan, Paris's radical historian, says this was really a settling of scores with old "red" Belleville, a reconquest of eastern Paris by "managers of domination," trying to erase inhabitants' past existence, especially their past "emotional experience," and cashing in on it.

Perec's project was based on individual memory and his

subjective recollections of this past existence. Nonetheless, he claimed it was different from autobiography. "It works like a sort of appeal to memory," he said, "because it's something that is shared. It starts out from a common memory, a collective memory," a past collective existence. Documenting real places—*lieux réels*—as neutral as possible, he says, lets us see how this collective memory is kept alive, how it might become a political tool, how we can remember aspects of the city that are threatened or have already been destroyed. Sites of past social struggles, even lost battles, maybe especially lost battles, might be remembered, used as grist for future campaigns, for future acts of remembrance, for keeping memory alive.

This isn't "official" collective memory being relayed, a past of presidents and mayors and famous individuals, of national events and wars. ("Napoleon, my ass," says Raymond Queneau's impish young heroine, Zazie.) Instead, it's ordinary aspects of everyday life, quietly acknowledged by ordinary people, expressive of shared identity. Collective memory is akin to an extended mind, stretching over time and space, an ongoing recollection of "what happens when nothing happens," as Perec liked to say. Plenty happens, of course, only so incrementally in daily life that we often don't see it, don't recognize it—until it's taken away, until it has gone.

PEREC USES A PECULIAR TERM to describe this sensibility: "infra-ordinary," the opposite of the extraordinary. It's another kind of anthropology, he says, not something exotic but *endotic*, a getting inside, of documenting the banal and the habitual, of what reoccurs each day, what people actually experience in their life in the city. It focuses closer to home, perhaps even takes people home—like the Métro. "The daily newspapers," says Perec, "talk of everything except the daily." It's always the big event, the untoward, the front-page splash, banner headlines. "Railway trains only begin to exist when they're derailed, and the more passengers killed the more the trains exist."

Behind the event, Perec says, there has to be "a fissure, a danger, as if life reveals itself only by way of the spectacular, as if what speaks, what is significant, is always abnormal: natural cataclysms or historical upheavals, social unrest, political scandals." (When the great photographer of ordinary daily life, André Kertész, quit Paris in 1936 for New York, his tender and poetic everyday images failed to grab the attention of major commercial magazines like *Life*; spectacular color shots took priority there, not monochrome street scenes where little seems to happen.)

In our haste to capture attention, Perec says, we leave aside the essential; we miss it. "What we need to question," he thinks, "is bricks, concrete, glass . . . our utensils, our tools, the way we spend our time, our rhythms. We live, true, we breathe, true; we walk, we open doors, we go down staircases, we sit at a table in order to eat, we lie on a bed in order to sleep. How? Where? When? Why? Describe your street. Describe another street. Compare." These questions might seem futile, he says, but "that's exactly what makes them just as essential, if not more so, as all the other questions by which we've tried in vain to lay hold on our truth."

Perec gives us some practical exercises to do when we're out drinking coffee in Starbucks or having a beer in a bar. It's an infra-ordinary methodological checklist. Get by a window, he says. "Observe the street. . . . Note down what you can see. Anything worthy of note going on. Do you know how to see what's worthy of note? Is there anything that strikes you? Nothing strikes you? You don't know how to see." Rather, he says, "you must set about it more slowly, almost stupidly. Force yourself to write down what is of no interest, what is most obvious, most common, most colorless . . . Make an effort to exhaust the subject, even if it seems grotesque, or pointless, or stupid. Force yourself to see more flatly. Detect a rhythm. Read what's written in the street. Decipher a bit of the city, deduce the obvious facts."

Daily newspapers talk of everything except the daily, everything except the stuff Perec wants us to emphasize. We might say the same thing about our urban policies. They likewise talk about everything but daily life, everything except the actual reality of people who live in cities. They feature little more than news of spectacular meta-projects, of "new science of cities," of catchy epithets that describe the new urban forms emerging over the past few decades: endless city, one-hundred-mile city, global city, megacity, arrival city, indistinguishable city, incorporated city. The common denominator isn't only that these projects and concepts wrench themselves out of everyday life, that they affirm the extraordinary over the ordinary; they've also become a field day for a primitive accumulation of "expert" knowledge and capital accumulation, driving a new capitalist growth sector that COVID appears to have reenergized: *urban solutionism*.

Solutionism invariably gravitates between triumphalism and dystopianism. On the one hand is triumphalism, a celebration of our urban order, a belief that cities hold the key to global economic well-being, indeed are the very motors of this well-being: 80 percent of global GDP, triumphalists note, is generated by cities. As such, urban solutionism must nurture and maximize this capacity. Its common thrust, engineered and endorsed by real estate professionals, architects, business chiefs, start-up CEOs, and government officials, is to exploit the business potential of every nook and cranny of urban life, privatize everyday life without ever noticing *everyday* everyday life. Little looks to have changed under COVID.

If anything, this orthodoxy has been absorbed into that other strand of urban policy, its less boosterist face: dystopianism. Here again, profiteers stalk the corridors of power, scaremongering for funds and fulminating against the Sodoms and Gomorrahs in our midst. Neo-Malthusian arguments prevail: urban regions are just too big, too overpopulated, and too environmentally hazardous. Cities wallow in squalor and decay and have too many people for the available resources. Hence the plethora of agencies and institutes, philanthropic foundations and think tanks that want to "help," that propose private sector-led partnerships to assist our tired and huddled masses.

They dream up vast new infrastructure and high-tech fixes, do everything except attack property speculation and impugn the market. They refuse to acknowledge resource scarcity as a socially produced reality, artificially created through access to wealth and monopoly power. Thus dystopians bemoan scarcity while triumphalists squander "scarce" resources, pouring them into edifices like Hudson Yards, into mega-projects built by "starchitects," doing this at a time when the public sector is forever under fire from austerity. Triumphalism and dystopianism feed off of one another, actively necessitate each other. They're different sides of the same capitalist urban coin. Either way, what we have here is a deadening conformity to an "extraordinary" urban order, a flattening of the city, together with a blindness to everyday urban people.

THERE'S A SHORT FILM AND interview with Georges Perec, made in 1976, available online at France's Institut national de l'audiovisuel (INA) (www.ina.fr). In the beginning, we see him atop the staircase at rue Vilin, clad in a vivid white parka coat, with its fur-lined collar, dreamily staring out over Paris. It's an epic viewpoint he has, a dramatic vista over the whole of the City

of Light. Up above, Perec liked to cite Raymond Queneau's funny expression: "The roofs of Paris, lying on their backs, with their little paws in the air." Moments later, we watch Perec descend the staircase and enter the run-down street he knew as a kid, soon standing in front of the decaying doorframe that was once his childhood home.

That spot up on rue Vilin's staircase is no more. Still, on a recent trip to Paris, where I went to finish this book, I tried to follow in Perec's footsteps, to find what remained of rue Vilin and stand approximately where he once stood. I sought a similar vantage point to survey Paris, wondering if the topography of what remained might let me mimic the top of old rue Vilin's staircase. Rue Vilin sort of still exists, though now it's a shaded pedestrian passageway, walled on one side by a 1980s brutalist four-story apartment block, looking rather moldy, off-white colored and splattered with graffiti. The building hasn't aged well.

You might say it's an abomination of urban design. The tree line is too close to the north-facing building. So, while the apartments have little curved balconies, they're unlikely ever to see light. And the street itself, or what remains of it, is uninviting,

little more than a darkened tunnel. Who would want to walk here? Little wonder there's nobody about. And without people, the more that graffiti will get splattered, and the less anybody will ever want to venture there. Jane Jacobs wouldn't have been impressed. It goes against her principal tenets of visibility and busyness. Nor is Eric Hazan, who's damning. Those responsible for these "urban warts," he says, should be publicly condemned. The architect who thought it up and who never likely even visited the site should be outed, along with the state officials who signed off the construction permit. Their names need to be posted somewhere on a neighborhood wall of shame, Hazan says, for everyone to see, their dastardly deeds remembered forevermore.

The street signage is there: RUE VILIN. I'm looking at it now. But it's hard to call it a street anymore. It's a stark contrast to the charm evident from those old films and photos of Perec's era. The line that was presumably once the old street peters out at Belleville Park's gates, turning cobbled as you cross its threshold. I wonder if these cobbles are the remains of rue Vilin's originals? The topography rises, as rue Vilin's once rose, only now it's punctuated by a series of steps, many uneven and broken down, a little worse for wear despite the fact they're not very old; the tree-lined corridor, leading you up to the summit of *la colline de Belleville*, is again dimly lit and bereft of people, threatening for the solitary stroller.

Near the top is a large modern glass building, *La maison de l'air*, abandoned and in a state of disrepair, its sidewalls daubed with graffiti. Until 2013, it was a neighborhood community and cultural space with an interesting-looking outdoor amphitheater, presumably the former site of al fresco theatrical performances. But everything looks sad and forlorn. On the door, a poster is pasted, notifying residents of a vote to be held in September 2022 on the *maison*'s future, whether a "participatory budget" might relaunch its activities.

At the side of the building, another set of steps takes you up higher again onto an observation area that opens out over the city, a glorious panorama of east, south, and west Paris. The Eiffel Tower, Pompidou Center, Notre Dame, Panthéon, and Montparnasse Tower dot the landscape, shimmering in the fierce heatwave we're experiencing. This is surely where Perec stood, the same elevation and vantage point. I've found it. For a while, I admire the view and think of him. Then I search for traces of the

in
the
part

man, any mention of him in the graffiti, on a poster somewhere, on a nearby wall, anything, any hint of Perec's past presence. Nothing.

Did I really expect anything? I remember what Henri Lefebvre once said: Perec was the most enigmatic young man he'd ever met. Lefebvre took Perec under his wing; Perec spent summers with Lefebvre at his house in Navarrenx, in the Pyrenean foothills. The old professor and the young novelist likely taught one another a few tricks. When the man who sleeps woke up, he read, like Perec himself, Lefebvre's treatise on everyday life. Everyday life was the standpoint from where Lefebvre constructed his maverick urban theory, just as it was the vantage point from where Perec constructed his idiosyncratic literature. Both got down into the neighborhoods; both knew how to think big while looking at the small, filling in larger context with particular meaning.

So, in a way, above, looking down on Paris, it's alien to Lefebvre and Perec's sensibility. They were much happier hanging out below, down at street level. High up is a conceptual vantage point that Lefebvre condemned, labeling it a "representation of space." Lefebvre formulated such a proposition to problematize how people with power and wealth conceive reality, how they literally and metaphorically look down upon it, envision from above the world we are compelled to live in down below. They do so because they have the authority and resources to convert their abstract, remote conceptions into real-life representations, into concrete and ideological manifestations. They make space subject to their own signs and codifications, to their own grandiose plans and world-historical paradigms. That modern apartment building along old rue Vilin is a quintessential representation of space, foisted down into lived experience, whether those who lived out that experience liked it or not.

Representations of space may be "abstract," Lefebvre says, may be conceived in business imaginations, in corporate conference rooms, at high-level consultations and on architects' drawing boards, but "abstract" is misleading: there's nothing abstract here, nothing abstract in the sense of something purely conceptual, existing only in the mind. This abstract is deeply and troublingly *real*, embodied in spaces like the world market, glass and steel, drab concrete and breezeblock, security zones and trade agreements. Abstract space has a very real social existence, just as abstract labor does, as interest rates and share prices do; it finds objective expression in specific buildings and housing markets, in activities and modes of market intercourse over and through space, especially through urban space.

Lefebvre knew the wealthy have everyday lives as well. They live in the lived realm like everybody else. But they function differently; that's his point. They are bearers of roles that affect ordinary people's everyday life in ways that are often detached from their rich, privileged everyday life. Lefebvre tries to figure this out in *The Production of Space* (1974), locating how different visions of spatial reality coexist and conflict. He insists that we all somehow "produce" space, yet we can't make that space in the same way or on equal terms. Power begins on an abstract plane and projects its conception down on us from above, making its abstraction concrete and material. Marx explains as much in a famous passage of *Kapital*: "A spider conducts operations which resemble those of the weaver, and a bee would put many a human architect to shame by the construction of its honeycomb cells. But what distinguishes the worst of architect from the best of bees is that the architect raises his structure in imagination before he erects it in reality. At the end of every labor process, a result emerges which had already been conceived . . . hence already existed ideally."

Since ordinary people usually don't have those means, they must start concrete and try to scale upward and outward, ideally,

realizing their abstract renderings as futuristic yearnings. In the
process, they, we, frequently fail, encounter barriers, political and
economic obstacles that prevent those projects from ever getting
realized let alone generalized. But could we reimagine another
urban policy, another municipal intervention that might mediate between these realms, that could keep the conceived and
the lived democratically together? A policy that conceives a big,
abstract, progressive ideal for the whole city yet ensures this ideal
is concrete and devolved, sensitive to each constituent piece of
the city, to the needs of each neighborhood and its denizens, to
each city within *the* city. It's like having your cake and eating it.
Or maybe it's like having a parallactic urban plan, seeing binocular, understanding the urban gestalt, looking over Paris like Perec
does, over any city, from on high, as I am now; only this isn't
some titanic authoritarian vision we're talking about, a Baron
Haussmann slashing through the cityscape with vicious saber
cuts, or a Robert Moses swinging his "meat axe."

It's more a reconciliation of the urban dialectic, the abstract
conjoined with the concrete, an appreciation of the city at its most
mundane lived level, like a stroll through one of Aragon's beloved
old arcades; a popular (not populist) conception of everyday life,
a sensitivity to the Surrealists' urging to foster the extraordinary
in the ordinary, to plan and factor in spontaneous novelty. For it's
impossible to work in the other direction: there can be no ordinary in the abstraction of the extraordinary, no lived life in those
abstract representations done from above, envisioned undemo-
cratically through power and money, in the Hudson Yards we see
everywhere around us. The sole possibility is the extraordinary
lying latent in the ordinary, in its teasing out, in nurturing and
preserving its unassumed thrill.

One of the twists in the photography of André Kertész is how
images taken from on high and seemingly extrapolated from daily

André Kertész
Perec

life aren't impositions, aren't done from a position of domination. They actually give us intimate perspectives on everyday private life, often on the private lives of people in public. Some of
Kertész's own favorites are taken from the top of stairwells, from
high balconies and windows, from rooftops; for years, he had a
bird's-eye view over Washington Square Park, from the balcony
of his own 12th-floor apartment on Fifth Avenue; his most sensitive representations of New York life are framed from this vantage point. In these photographs, like the cover shot of this very
book, individuals and clustered groups, both stationary and in
motion, are pictured from afar. Yet somehow, they seem so close,
so human and real, so relatable and touchable. We can almost
eavesdrop on their conversations and personal silences, on their
innermost thoughts. (Perhaps, too, we can witness some innate
sense not only of spatial ordering but also of social distancing, a
kind of spontaneous human spacing between people.)

Kertész was a visionary image-maker who saw the big story in
the little picture. He captured in microcosm the *totality* of urban
daily life, its parts within a well-chosen whole, little trees inside
the great enchanted wood. A parallactic urban plan might similarly try to bring to policy Kertész's poetic eye for people. Why
shouldn't policy be poetic as well as pragmatic, all-embracing yet
sensitive to concrete detail? And why can't responsible planners,
architects, municipal officials, and state "representatives"—all
those concerned with urban development—focus on neighborhoods? Get out from behind their desks and computer screens
and venture into streets and cafés, into the real everyday life of
people, and engage in endotic anthropology? With notebook in
hand, a keen eye and curiosity for people, and a willingness to
walk the streets, they can look and learn, take note of the infra-
ordinary as Perec suggests we should take note. They might
detect the rhythms and patterns and needs of people on the

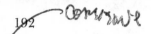

ground, really look and listen, decipher what's going on. They might become real representatives of a lived urban strategy, and their inventory the starting point for a citizens' dialogue, for a reconciliation of that other breach in urban political life: between representation and participation.

Belleville isn't a bad place to ponder this. At the corner of rue de Tourtille and rue Ramponeau, in the heart of the neighborhood, just a few minutes' walk from the Parc de Belleville, the last barricade of the Commune fell. The barricades went up seventy-three days earlier, and the Communards' direct participations were evident enough; effective enough, we might say, to establish new, federated forms of democratic representation. Elected representatives held mandates in neighborhoods and workplaces. Experimental representative democracy was invented from militant participation. When the last Belleville barricade was dismantled, so, too, was the rare glimpse of representative-participatory democracy.

The crossroads of rue de Tourtille and rue Ramponeau still looks pretty working class. Both streets aren't very wide. The fabric is old, nicely frayed. It's early morning and quiet, and I'm standing alone looking at a large mural of Germaine Tillion, "*résistante, ethnologue,*" at the intersection of the two streets, probably on the precise spot where the Communards' barricade once spanned. In the 1940s, Germaine Tillion fought for the French Resistance movement, was betrayed, got sent off to Ravensbrück concentration camp, where she secretly documented its harrowing conditions. But somehow, she survived, hatched a daring great escape, made it out to tell her story and live on. As a student, Tillion had studied with the anthropologist Marcel Mauss, best known for his book *The Gift* (1925); throughout the 1930s, she worked as an ethnologist in Algeria. After the war, she returned to Algeria and established close links with the FLN, becoming a staunch anti-colonialist and supporter

of Algerian independence. Tillion was born in Allègre, a village in the Haute-Loire I know very well; I began my book *The Wisdom of Donkeys* (2008) there. She lived to be one hundred and was an active freedom fighter and advocate of social justice till the very end of her long and eventful life, fêted and inspiringly remembered in Belleville.

But looking at her mural now and thinking about resistance today—thinking about *résistantes* and *résistants* the world over, about participation and representation (and lack of it)—I'm skeptical about the nature of barricades in cities. I wonder whether they're somehow retrogressive, put up to defend property rather than inform progressive government. Perhaps barricades shouldn't so much go up in city life as be torn down, those barricades as barriers, the highways that cut off neighborhoods from one another, that sever centers from peripheries, rich from poor, whites from blacks. I'm talking about those *Boulevards Périphériques* in our lives, interstate highways that plow through cities. I'm talking about walls and fencing, frequently barbed-wired fencing, that keep people in as well as out.

I'm thinking about resistance where barricades aren't

"manned" inwardly, erected to defend. I'm thinking about flexible and portable activism, outward-looking and affirmative; a progressive activism that moves between nodes, that occasionally disrupts and blocks yet at the same time fosters new life within. I'm thinking about mobilizations that tear down real or imagined walls of fear, in the street and in people's heads. I'm thinking about how new spaces of encounter might be formed, new agoras for assemblies of the people. This is what resistance might mean today: something positive, a new gift for one another to share, a new prophylactic against future plagues.

All around Belleville's streets, there are assorted *affiches*, posters pasted onto walls, each flagging up some progressive political cause. They're part of infra-ordinary life. Many politick for immigrants' and housing rights; others publicize mobilizations against the extreme Right—"*contra l'extreme droite et son monde.*" "*Clément est toujours présent,*" one says, highlighting a demo that took place in June 2022, commemorating Clément Méric, a nineteen-year-old militant anti-fascist who, nine years ago, was shot dead by a neo-Nazi. Elsewhere are posters of Jean-Luc Mélenchon and "*L'Union Populaire,*" the New Popular Union of Greens and Socialists (NUPES) who recently gained ground at France's National Assembly, acquiring sufficient seats to prevent *La Macronie* from taking over everywhere, equally offering a bulwark against Marine Le Pen. *Popular Union* is one big idea for the future, a beacon of hope for the Left in a global landscape where "popular" has hitherto meant hopelessly Right.

Walking along the Boulevard de Belleville, through its twice-weekly (Tuesdays and Fridays) open-air market, teeming with immigrant street life, I weave in and out of people. I'm listening to all kinds of languages getting bawled out by vendors and customers alike. I feel heartened, grateful to be in a big city, glad I'm alive in the open air, glad everyday life is ordinary, glad there are still progressive people fighting the good fight, pasting up posters, organizing demos, sometimes making the ordinary feel a little bit extraordinary. I'm glad I remember Perec's *Man Who Sleeps*, too, remember him waking up, jaunting around Belleville as the sun goes down, not far from where I am now, as he returns into the land of the living.

"*Tu n'es pas mort*," the narrator's voiceover says, transcribing what's going through the protagonist's head, "*tu n'es pas devenu fou, tu n'as rien appris sinon que la solitude n'apprend rien, que l'indifférence n'apprend rien . . . C'est un jour comme celui-ci, un peu plus tard, un peu plus tôt, que tout recommence, que tout commence, que tout continue. Cesse de parler comme un homme qui rêve . . . Regarde!*" It's a beautiful conclusion, maybe even a fitting ending for a book: "You aren't dead, you haven't become mad, you've learned nothing, other than solitude teaches you nothing, that indifference teaches nothing . . . It's a day like any other, a little later, a little earlier, where everything recommences, everything begins, everything continues. Stop talking like a man who dreams," who's asleep. "Look!"

ACKNOWLEDGMENTS

My gratitude goes out to Michael Yates and Martin Paddio
at Monthly Review Press, such pleasures to work with and so
accomplished at what they do. Thank you both sincerely.